BIBLICAL ETHICS

**Other Evangelical Training Association
books from Crossway Books**

Exploring the Old Testament
Exploring the New Testament
Exploring Church History
Exploring the Basics of the Bible
Evidence and Truth
Biblical Truth
The One True God: Father, Son, and Holy Spirit
Growing Toward Spiritual Maturity

BIBLICAL ESSENTIALS

BIBLICAL ETHICS

Choosing Right in a World Gone Wrong

JAMES P. ECKMAN

CROSSWAY BOOKS

A DIVISION OF
GOOD NEWS PUBLISHERS
WHEATON, ILLINOIS

Cover design: Josh Dennis

Cover photo: Adobe Image Library

First printing 2004

Printed in the United States of America

Library of Congress Cataloging-in-Publication Data
Eckman, James P. (James Paul)
   Biblical ethics : choosing right in a world gone wrong / James P. Eckman.
      p. cm. — (Biblical essentials series)
   Originally published: Wheaton, Ill. : Evangelical Training Association,
© 1999.
   Includes bibliographical references.
   ISBN 1-58134-572-0 (alk. paper)
   1. Ethics in the Bible. 2. Christian ethics—Biblical teaching. I. Title.
II. Series.
BS680.E84E33   2004
241—dc22   2003021393

VP		13	12	11	10	09	08	07	06	05	04
15	14	13	12	11	10	9	8	7	6	5	4	3	2	1

CONTENTS

1

Ethics: An Introduction

IN MODERN CULTURE the terms *ethics* and *morals* are virtual synonyms. Quite frankly the confusion over the interchangeableness of these two terms is understandable, but it is wrong. From history we learn that the two words have different meanings. *Ethics* comes from the Greek word *ethos*, meaning a "stall" for horses, a place of stability and permanence. The word *morality* came from *mores*, which describes the shifting behavioral patterns of society.

Ethics is what is normative, absolute. It refers to a set of standards around which we organize our lives and from which we define our duties and obligations. It results in a set of imperatives that establishes acceptable behavior patterns. It is what people *ought* to do. By contrast, morality is more concerned with what people *do*. It describes what people are already doing, often regardless of any absolute set of standards.[1]

We now see the problem of the modern human condition. When ethics and morality are confused and mixed, the result is that the culture makes the norms. The standards become relativistic and changing. That which is the norm is identified with that which is the absolute. The absolute standards are destroyed by the fluid nature of the culture. Relativism triumphs over the absolute.

This is where modern culture is today. We determine the norm of human behavior through statistical studies, like the Kinsey report[2] did on human sexuality. Behavior the Bible condemns (e.g., adultery, homosexuality) is practiced widely, statistical analysis demonstrates. Therefore, since this behavior is widely practiced, that becomes society's norm and therefore its ethical standard. Ethics becomes a relativistic, floating set of patterns that determines our duty and obligation. Nothing is absolute, and nothing is forever. What the culture thought was nailed down is not. It is as fluid as a changing river.

The Bible will have none of this. The deep-seated conviction of the Christian is the proposition that God exists and that He has revealed Himself. That revelation is verbal and propositional; it is contained in the Bible. That revelation contains the absolute set of standards rooted in God's character and will. He knows what is best for us because He created us and He redeemed us. Therefore, His verbal revelation contains the absolute standard on which we base our lives and construct our duties and obligations to the family, the church, and the state.

To God ethics is not a set of fluid standards. It is a set of absolutes that reflects His character and defines human duty. He wants us to love Him and love our neighbor as ourselves. This twin injunction is a powerful example of duty to God and duty to other humans. It is an imperative for all humans. It constitutes a supernatural window into what is good, right, just, and perfect. As Erwin Lutzer has argued, "We must be willing to set aside temporarily the question of what actions *are* right or wrong to focus on a more basic question: What *makes* an action right or wrong?"[3] That is why God has the right to say to us, "Be holy for I am holy." He, the Creator, sets the standard against which we must measure all behavior.

WHY STUDY ETHICS?

There are several reasons for the study of ethics. Each is separate, and yet they overlap. The reasons I offer here are not exhaustive. Rather, they offer compelling evidence that the study of ethics is desperately needed in the church. Few Christians know how to think about the major cultural issues ripping apart our society. Instead, they often sit on the sidelines and allow non-Christians to dominate the discussion on abortion, human sexuality, the role of the state, issues of war, and the environment. Few seem ready to give a defense of the absolute standards of God's Word. This book gives Christians a starting point for thinking and acting on the basis of God's revelation. It enables believers to speak ethical truth to the culture.

The first reason for a study of ethics is that Western culture has relinquished any absolute framework for thinking about ethical standards. One powerful example of this is bioethics. Medical technology is moving so fast that ethical considerations usually are subsumed by the practical. But this is not right!

How should we think about the issue of using animal organs in human beings? Should we place a baboon's heart in a human being? Should we place animal tissue in humans? Should we use the cells of an anencephalic baby in a human? Should we use *in vitro* fertilization to help infertile couples have a baby? Should we clone human beings? Should we use gender selection when parents want to choose whether to have a boy or girl?

All of these medical practices are being done or can be done. Does the Bible say anything about these issues? As later chapters in this book show, the Bible does speak to these questions and provides a set of standards and principles to guide humans in making these difficult decisions. Christians *must* be involved in this debate over bioethics (see chapter 6).

A second reason focuses on the "slippery slope" nature of so many ethical questions. Consider abortion. In 1973 when the Supreme Court ruled that a woman could have an abortion based on the implied right of privacy it said was in the United States Constitution, no one realized how powerful this doctrine would become. This implied right reframed the whole abortion issue. Now the culture no longer focuses on the rights of the baby; instead, the entire debate focuses on the rights of the woman to the total exclusion of the baby's rights (see chapter 4).

That same logic now informs the euthanasia debate. The discussion focuses on the right of the person to die with dignity. Doctor-assisted suicide is now sanctioned in some states using the implied right of privacy that formerly sanctioned the practice of abortion. A person who is ill and no longer desires to live, based on the implied right of privacy, can receive assistance from a doctor to commit suicide (see chapter 5).

Ethical issues feed on one another. The logic of one is used by the culture to frame the debate on the other. Christians must understand this process, or they will have no impact on the debates about life currently raging in our culture. The slippery slope nature of ethics without divine revelation explains why what was once unthinkable becomes debatable, and soon becomes culturally acceptable. We must come to terms with this aspect of humanistic ethics.

Third, Christians must understand the integrated nature of ethical issues. Most Christians do not know how to use the Bible to approach contemporary ethical issues. For many the Bible seems irrelevant. But this sad state of affairs cannot continue. Christians must learn to think biblically and Christianly about ethical concerns.

The Bible is God's Word. In 2 Timothy Paul argues that the Bible equips for every good work and is beneficial for correction, rebuking, and training in righteousness (3:16-17). Obviously, studying the Word is necessary for ethical decision-making. God's Word gives God's view of life and His absolute standards. One cannot assume that the baby growing in the mother's womb has no value to God. If He is the Creator, as the Bible declares Him, then life is of infinite value to Him. Humans, regardless of any discussion of rights, do not have permission to wantonly destroy life. To do so violates one of God's absolute standards rooted in His character. This process of discerning God's mind on an issue, developing a principle from it, and then reaching an ethical position is the process defended in this book. The Bible is not irrelevant to ethics. Instead, it is the foundation for ethics.

Fourth, many Christians know where they stand on certain ethical issues, but they cannot defend their positions. This book charts a biblical defense for each position presented. For example, most Christians believe that homosexuality is wrong. That is an ethical judgment. But why is it wrong? It is not much help to simply state, "The Bible says it is wrong." Perhaps a better defense is to root the ethical belief about human sexuality in the creation ordinance of God.

God created humanity in two grand streams—male and female. In Genesis 2 He makes clear that His design is that the male and female marry and "become one flesh." This solves the challenge of human loneliness and isolation that Adam experienced. Eve, as God's gift to the man, serves as his spiritual equal (both are in His image, Gen. 1:26-27) but yet his complement. This complementary relationship defines the basis of human sexuality, because men and women rule the creation as God's stewards and populate His planet. Human sexuality relates to the essence of human responsibility—ruling God's creation together as a complementary whole, male and female together (Gen. 1:26ff.). Whenever Jesus or Paul deals with marriage or human sexuality, each goes back to this creation ordinance of God (Matt. 19; 1 Cor. 7). Here we see God's ideal for human sexual relationships, and there is no room for homosexuality in this ordinance (see chapter 7).

Ethical decision-making is a part of everyday life. Christians must not only know what they believe, but they must likewise explain why. This book gives Christians a resource to define ethics as absolute standards that result in proper duty and obligation to God and fellow humans. The next chapter surveys the ethical options for

Christians, defending the position of ethical absolutes as the only biblical option.

FOR FURTHER DISCUSSION

1. Summarize the difference between morality and ethics.
2. What is the result of the confusion of ethics and morality?
3. How does God's revelation impact the view of absolute ethics?
4. List and briefly explain the four reasons for a study of ethics.

2

Ethical Options
for the Christian

THE THESIS OF this book is that ethics must be rooted in the proposition that ethical absolutes exist. Those absolutes are based on God's moral law revealed in His Word. God may be approached and His revelation understood through intellectual analysis. This claim is uniquely Christian and central to reconciliation with ethical absolutes. But before this absolute moral law is examined, the present culture's penchant for relativism needs discussion. This is necessary because relativistic ethical systems are inadequate moral guides. Why is this so?

CULTURAL RELATIVISM

Consider the option of cultural relativism. This view argues that whatever a cultural group approves of becomes right; whatever the group disapproves of is wrong. Since there are no fixed principles to guide developing moral codes, culture determines what is right and wrong. Every culture develops its own moral standards, and no other culture has the right to judge another's value system.

Consider the consequences of cultural relativism. The existence of varying cultural norms is undeniable. Whether these cultural differences ought to exist or whether all the moral viewpoints of the culture are equal must be settled by some other means. There simply must be something transcendent to settle these cultural differences. Furthermore, if culture decides the validity of moral behavior, we really cannot condemn any acceptable action within its own culture. For example, the Nazis were acting quite consistently within their cultural worldview. They believed Jews were a threat to their perfect Aryan race. Therefore, to rid European civilization of Jews was logically consistent within their cultural norms. Following cultural relativism, can Nazism be condemned?

Recent developments in higher education indicate another consequence of cultural relativism. Some students are unwilling to oppose great moral horrors (including human sacrifice, ethnic cleansing, and slavery) because they think no one has the right to criticize the moral views of another group or culture. Professor Robert Simon, who has been teaching philosophy for twenty years at Hamilton College in Clinton, New York, indicates that his students acknowledge the Holocaust occurred but cannot bring themselves to say that killing millions of people was wrong. Between 10 percent and 20 percent deplore what the Nazis did, but their disapproval is expressed as a matter of taste or personal preference, not of moral judgment. One student told Simon, "Of course I dislike the Nazis, but who is to say they are wrong?"

Another professor, Kay Haugaard of Pasadena College in California, wrote of a literature student who said of human sacrifice, "I really don't know. If it was a religion of long standing . . ." Haugaard was stunned that her student could not make a moral judgment. "This was a woman who wrote passionately of saving the whales, of concern for the rainforests, of her rescue and tender care of a stray dog."[1]

Cultural relativism can also lead to individual relativism. Truth in today's world is relegated to the individual or the group. What is true for one is not necessarily true for another. Truths for two different groups are equally valid, for they are equally based on personal outlook. The result of this ludicrous situation reminds one of the book of Judges: "Every man did what was right in his own eyes" (17:6). Individual relativism leads to social and ethical anarchy.

In the final analysis, cultural relativism propagates an unacceptable inconsistency. Denying the existence of all moral absolutes, the system wants to proclaim its own absolute—culture![2] The argument of the ethical relativist can be summarized in three propositions:

• What is considered morally right and wrong varies from society to society, so that there are no universal moral standards held by all societies.

• Whether or not it is right for an individual to act in a certain way depends on or is relative to the society to which he or she belongs.

• Therefore, there are no absolute or objective moral standards that apply to all people everywhere and at all times.[3]

The fallacy of absolutizing culture is exposed the moment sin enters into the discussion. Because sin is rebellion against God, one should not expect to see consistency of moral standards across various cultures, despite near universal condemnation of murder and incest, for example. The struggle to enforce even the standards against murder and incest is further evidence of the human need for redemption. It does not invalidate the ethical absolutes revealed in God's Word.

SITUATION ETHICS

Another option is situation ethics, popularized by Joseph Fletcher.[4] The core of his argument centers on the elimination of absolute moral principles because they place themselves over people. The only absolute that can be affirmed is love. But how is this universal of love defined? For Fletcher it must be defined in a utilitarian sense. Any action that produces more pleasure and less pain, the greatest good for the greatest number, is the "loving" thing to do. In other words, as Lutzer echoes, the end justifies the means.[5] In its utilitarian understanding of "love," adultery or lying could be justified.

In Fletcher's world, if a husband is married to an invalid, it would be loving for him to have an adulterous affair with another woman because his needs cannot be met by his wife. It is likewise loving for a woman to have an abortion because an unwanted or unintended baby should never be born. But this is biblically indefensible. Who decides what is loving? Who determines the definition of the "greatest good"? You are back to a subjectivism, where each person ultimately decides on his or her own definition of "good" and "loving."

BEHAVIORISM

A third ethical option is a product of behavioral psychology. Whether it is through genetics or the environment, humans are products of forces beyond their control, this position argues. Therefore, moral values and ethical issues are simply the product of genetic makeup or of environmental factors. The result is that people are not responsible for personal behavior.

One of the greatest proponents of behaviorism was the late B. F. Skinner,[6] famed psychologist from Harvard. Following his work with pigeons, Skinner believed that he could modify the behavior of any human. He argued that ethics are entirely based on responses to the conditioning factors of the environment. Human freedom and dignity are outmoded concepts that must be discarded if the human race is to survive. Utilizing the manipulative and conditioning techniques so central to behaviorism, Skinner maintained that "man has yet to discover what man can do for man." We must be willing to surrender human freedom and jettison human dignity if the race is to survive.

The Bible will have none of this. It declares that humans are responsible for their actions (Rom. 1—3). Although a factor, a person's environment does not totally explain a person's actions. To excuse someone's actions as an exclusive product of environmental conditioning flies in the face of the biblical doctrine of sin. Humans, because they are in rebellion against God, are guilty of sin and in need of redemption. No one is ever going to stand before God and offer an acceptable behaviorist response to explain his or her sin.

A CASE FOR ETHICAL ABSOLUTES

Erwin Lutzer makes this compelling argument: "If naturalism is false and if theism is true, and therefore God is responsible for all that is, then revelation is possible. And if revelation is possible, absolute standards are possible, should the Deity choose to make them known."[7]

Has, then, God chosen to make them known? The resounding answer is yes. He has chosen to reveal Himself in His Son (Heb. 1:1-4), through His creation (Ps. 19; Rom. 1:18ff.), and through His Word (Ps. 119; 2 Tim. 3:16; 2 Pet. 1:21). We know about the Son through the Word. These propositional truths form the basis for ethical absolutes.

What are these propositional truths that constitute the ethical framework for the Christian?

1. *God's moral revelation in His Word is an expression of His own nature.* He is holy, and therefore He insists that His human creatures also meet that standard. If they do not, judgment results. Hence, the vital nature of Jesus' substitutionary atonement. Appropriating that atoning work by faith makes the human holy in God's sight. The same could be argued for ethical standards of truth, beauty, love, life, and sexuality.

2. *God's moral and ethical system consists of more than external conformity to His moral code; it centers on conformity with internal issues of motivation and personal attitudes.* Jesus' teaching in the Sermon on the Mount presses this point. The ethical standard of prohibiting adultery involves more than simply the external act; it also involves lusting with the heart after another person (Matt. 5:27-28). The ethical standard of prohibiting murder involves more than the external act;

it also involves the standard of bitterness, hatred, and anger in the heart (Matt. 5:21-22).

3. *God provides the absolute criteria for determining the value of human beings.* Because physical, economic, mental, and social/cultural criteria are all arbitrary and relative, they are inadequate for assigning value to humans. For example, Francis Crick, the Nobel prize-winning biologist, has advocated legislation mandating that newborn babies would not be considered legally alive until they were two days old and had been certified as healthy by medical examiners. Former Senator Charles Percy of Illinois argued that abortion is a good deal for the tax-payer because it is considerably cheaper than welfare. Winston L. Duke, a nuclear physicist, stated that reason should define a human being as life that demonstrates self-awareness, volition, and rationality. Since some people do not manifest these qualities, some are not human. Finally, Ashley Montagu, a British anthropologist, believes that a baby is not born human. Instead, it is born with a capacity for becoming human as he or she is molded by social and cultural influences.[8]

God created humans in His image (Gen. 1:26ff.) and established His absolute criteria for assigning value to human beings. Being in the image of God means that humans resemble God. Humans possess self-consciousness, self-will, and moral responsibility, as does God. What humans lost in the Fall (Gen. 3) was righteousness, holiness, and knowledge; these are renewed in the Christian as he or she is conformed to the image of Christ. Theology calls these communicable attributes (e.g., love, holiness, mercy, etc.) as they are present and possible in humans.

Being in His image also means that humans represent God. God's purpose in creating human beings in His image is functional (Gen. 1:26-27). Humans have the responsibility of dominion over creation and of being fruitful and multiplying. Humans represent God as His stewards over all creation. This concept is emphasized in Genesis 2 and reiterated in Psalms 8 and 110. Human beings are God's vice-regents over all creation with power to control, regulate, and harness its potential. The Fall did not abolish this stewardship. Instead, Satan is the usurper and enemy of humans in this dominion status. Humans live out of harmony with themselves and with nature. Created to rule, men and women find that the crown has fallen from their brows.[9]

As Francis Schaeffer argued, "Unlike the evolutionary concept of an impersonal beginning plus time plus chance, the Bible gives an

account of man's origin as a finite person made in God's image. . . ."[10]
Humans have personality, dignity, and value and are superbly unique.
Unlike the naturalistic worldview, where there is no qualitative difference between human and other life, the Bible declares the infinite value
of all humans. This proposition forms the basis for examining all ethical issues that relate to life and provides the foundation for Christians
to uphold God's view of human beings in an increasingly pagan culture.

FOR FURTHER DISCUSSION

1. Define and give a reasoned critique of the following ethical options:
   • cultural/ethical relativism
   • situation ethics
   • behaviorism
2. How does the proposition that God has revealed Himself relate to
   ethical absolutes?
3. What can we say about God's standard concerning the following:
   • The external and internal dimensions of moral/ethical behavior
   • The value of human life to God
   • The image-of-God concept
   • The created-person concept
4. On what basis can we say that humans are of infinite value to God?
   Explain.

3

How Should a Christian Relate to Culture?

THE BIBLE WARNS against worldliness and the devastating consequences of following the world rather than Christ (James 4). From the Old Testament we see that the children of Israel got into big trouble when they imitated their pagan neighbors and brought their altars and images into the temple. Yet Christians are somehow to be in the world, but not of the world (John 17:14-18). Christians have been removed from the world's power at conversion (Gal. 6:14), and because the cross established a judicial separation between believers and the world, Christians are citizens of a new kingdom (Phil. 3:20). The Bible both discourages absolute physical separation from the people of the world (1 Cor. 5:9-10) and instructs believers to witness to this world (John 17:18), all the while avoiding the influence of the world (James 1:27; 1 Cor. 7:31; Rom. 12:2; 1 John 2:15). How does one resolve this tension?

This is a profoundly important question for those who hold to ethical absolutes. In a culture that is increasingly pagan and relativistic, how one "speaks" Christianity to the culture is critical. Should Christians separate from the culture and live in isolation? Should Christians seek to accommodate completely to the culture and seek to influence its institutions and values from the inside? Or should Christians try to transform the culture by seeking to control its institutions and claim each for Christ? Historical examples for each approach are readily available from church history and are present today in our world. The goal of this chapter is to examine and evaluate each model biblically.[1]

THE SEPARATIONAL MODEL

The separational model of relating to culture argues that Christians must withdraw from any involvement in the world. There is an antithesis between the kingdom of God and the kingdom of this world, and the choice is clear— withdraw. Clear biblical examples of this choice are Noah (whom God called out of the culture before He destroyed it), Abram (called to separate from pagan Mesopotamia), and Moses (called to separate from idolatrous Egypt). The New Testament buttresses this conviction with verses such as Matthew 6:24 ("No one can serve two masters. . . ."), 1 Peter 2:11, and 1 John 2:15. For this model, the church of Jesus Christ is a counterculture that lives by kingdom principles. She is to have nothing to do with this world.

One historical example of this model centers on the church before Constantine's critical decree in A.D. 313. During that time, Christians refused to serve in the Roman army, to participate in pagan entertainment, and to bow to Caesar as lord. Christians were antagonistic and separated from the culture and yet sought to win unbelievers to Christ.

Another historical example is Anabaptism, exemplified in the various Mennonite and Amish groups of the sixteenth century, many of whom continue today. For them there is an absolute antithesis between the kingdom of God and this world. This enmity necessitates a rejection of the church-state concept—the revolutionary center of their worldview. The church, in their view, is a free association of believers; there is no "established" state church. Religious liberty, nonresistance, often pacifism, and refusal to take vows and oaths separate these communities from their culture. Isolated and separate, these groups engage in social service to further Christ's kingdom on earth.

A final historical example was the Christian community movement in the 1960s, when Christian communes dotted the American and European religious landscape. Clearly countercultural, these groups believed that the church had become hopelessly secularized. Therefore, Christianity needed to get back to the book of Acts where resources were shared, lifestyles were simple, and believers were clearly separate from the hostile culture. This alternative way, rooted in a radical separation, would lead the church back to its roots and to revival.

How should we think about the separational model? In a culture that is increasingly pagan and antagonistic, Christianity offers some appealing options. This model stresses the "otherworldly" character of a genuinely biblical Christianity and calls people to recognize that "this world is not my home," as we often sing. After all, Jesus radically rejected the status quo of His culture and died as a result.

Yet this model has serious dangers that necessitate its rejection as a viable option. First, separatism can quickly lead to asceticism, a lifestyle of self-denial that ends up denying the goodness of God's creation. From God's declaration in Genesis 1 that all of His creation is "good," to Paul's powerful affirmation that everything is created by God, and nothing is to be rejected (1 Tim. 4:4), the Bible condemns all tendencies toward an asceticism that denies creation's innate goodness.

Second, this model easily produces a dangerous sacred/secular dichotomy. The Bible clearly rejects the compartmentalization of life into things that are sacred and those that are secular. For the Christian, everything is sacred. Paul writes in 1 Corinthians 10:31 that the believer is to "do all to the glory of God." Finally, this model can lead to a complete withdrawal from culture, something clearly condemned in the Bible. In 1 Corinthians 5:9-11 Paul chastises the Corinthians for misunderstanding his admonition about disciplining the wayward brother. He says they incorrectly processed his teaching about not associating with sinners. The only way to completely avoid unbelievers, as they seemed to take Paul's instruction, was to die, and that is not what he had in mind. So the separational model is inadequate for the believer.

THE IDENTIFICATIONAL MODEL

Accommodation to the culture is the key word for this model—to live both in the kingdom of God and in the world. God works in the world both through the state and through the church. The believer, therefore, has a dual commitment to both. Identifying with, participating in, and working within all cultural institutions (e.g., business, government, law) is part of the mandate for the Christian. Christians are, therefore, to live both in the kingdom of God and the kingdom of this world.

Biblical examples of this model abound. Joseph rose to the top of ancient Egypt, serving as a sort of prime minister (Gen. 41:41-43). Similarly, Daniel played key political and advisory roles in the empires of both Babylon and Persia (Dan. 6:1-4). Jesus identified with the world, eating and drinking with tax collectors and assorted sinners. He clearly did not separate from the world, for He was a friend of Nicodemus and associated with key officials in the Roman army (e.g., the centurion). Finally, the book of Acts records apostles associating with the Ethiopian eunuch and Cornelius, another Roman official. Paul, in Romans 13:1-7, illustrates the role of the state as a clear sphere of God's work.

Historical examples are likewise numerous. After Constantine's decree in A.D. 313, the church-state dynamic changed. He restored church property. Bishops became equal with Roman officials. Over time the church became wealthy and powerful. Christianity became popular, the "in thing" for the empire. Complacency resulted. The church's power became political, and through the medieval period (A.D. 500-1500) it gained immense prestige and dominance. In fact, during the papacy of Innocent III (early 1200s), the church in effect ruled Western Europe.

Another example is modern civil religion, which sees the nation-state as ordained by God for a special redemptive mission. American religious leaders like Jonathan Edwards, Charles Finney, and Lyman Beecher believed that God chose America to be the savior of the world, a chosen people to accomplish redemptive purposes for all humanity. God's kingdom, they argued, would come first to America and then would spread through the rest of the world. Manifest Destiny, which defined American foreign policy in the pre-Civil War period, saw America's institutions as ideal, and God destined that those institutions be spread through North America. Such thinking had its origins in civil religion and partially explains the Mexican-American War (1846-1848) and other forms of expansionism. Similar arguments could be made about expansionism in the late nineteenth century, specifically the Spanish-American War of 1898.

As we evaluate the identificational model, its strengths are clear. It emphasizes the "this-worldly" character of the Christian life. There is much in this world that can and should be affirmed because it is ulti-mately good. This model calls people to recognize that there is impor-tance and good in this world now. It likewise affirms that God is at work in and through the cultural institutions—the state, business, and even the arts. A Christian can identify and find benefit in each of these institutions.

However, the weaknesses of this model are glaring. Its principal danger is that it can lull the Christian into complacency, into blindness toward the influence of evil in the culture's institutions. Anyone involved in politics knows that it is the greatest test of one's faith to work in politics. Evil is always present, and the pressure to compromise one's convictions is ever present. This model can also lead to an uncrit-ical acceptance of prevailing cultural practices and attitudes. Particularly in democracies where majority rule is so prevalent, pres-sures are strong to go with polling data as the basis for decision-mak-ing. The more Christians identify with the institutions, the more the institutions influence the Christian. Contemporary society is more permissive than that of the past, and the evangelical community is being affected by that permissiveness.

Finally, this model can lead to a loss of the church's prophetic stance. The church can almost become "married to the culture." A disastrous example comes from Nazi Germany. The church was crying, "better Hitler than Stalin," and uncritically embraced Hitler's state as a matter of expediency. The same happened in American culture, especially to justify the Mexican-American War and aspects of the Spanish-American War. This model has the danger, then, of producing a complacent and soft Christianity.

THE TRANSFORMATIONAL MODEL

This model takes the transforming power of Christ and applies it to culture. Despite the fallen nature of humanity and the subsequent curse on creation, Jesus' death, burial, and resurrection reversed the curse for both humans and culture. There is now hope of human release from the bondage to sin and for creation as well. This truth is the center of ancient Israel's hope that the world would be restored (Isa. 65) and of the New Testament's focus on Christ's redemptive work (Rom. 5:12-21). Romans 8:19-22 also emphasizes the complete remaking of creation from sin's curse. This hope is easily translated into an optimism about culture's transformation.

Historical examples of this model center on the transforming work of the gospel in a geographical area. During the Reformation, John Calvin's Geneva reflected this transforming power. Calvin taught the total lordship of Christ, that it extended to the state and to economics. Therefore, the government of Geneva experienced radical reform and pursued righteousness in making and enforcing its laws. Work to Calvin and Geneva was a God-ordained vocation, whatever its specific nature. The city, therefore, experienced a remarkable economic transformation as well. A similar process of change characterized the Puritan colony of Massachusetts Bay in the 1600s. The Puritans sought to bring all aspects of their culture into conformity with God's revelation. It was a great cultural transformation.

There is much to affirm in this model. It recognizes the gospel's power to change both individuals and their culture. It is common sense to expect that when a person trusts Christ, his or her lifestyle and culture will therefore change. Ultimately, nothing in culture is immune from the gospel's impact. Likewise, this model calls on Christians to recognize their responsibility to work toward the day when God's kingdom will come to earth and justice will rule (Amos 5:15, 24).

There are, however, several serious shortcomings with this model. The transformationist can neglect the radical nature of sin's devastation. Humans remain enslaved to sin, and even believers struggle daily with its power. Scripture abounds with warnings about how subtle and powerful the enemies of the world, the flesh, and the devil really are. In addition, the transformational model can promote an unbiblical optimism, a near utopianism. The Bible rejects such optimism apart from the return of Jesus Christ. Humans, even those regenerated by faith, always struggle with sin, and only when Jesus returns will the victory over evil be complete. Therefore the transformational model must also be rejected.

THE INCARNATIONAL MODEL

Robert Webber[2] proposes a synthesis of all three models as the best alternative. His proposal is modeled after Jesus, for He separated from the evils of His culture, identified with its institutions and people, and yet sought to transform it from the inside out. By adding humanity to His deity, Jesus identified with the world in its social order—its people and its customs. The church is to do something similar. At bottom, this is the heart of Christ's admonition that we are to be in the world but not of it. Yet Christ separated Himself from the evil distortions of the created order. He had nothing to do with the wrong use of wealth, social position, or political power. Finally, through His death, burial, and resurrection, He broke the power of sin and Satan and guaranteed the world's transformation when He returns in glory and power. Similarly, the church is to move culture's institutions toward genuine biblical righteousness, all the while anticipating Christ's final transforming work when He returns.

How does the believer live out Webber's incarnational model? First, the Christian always lives with tension, the tension between what is transformable and that from which he or she must separate. For example, there are many good structures in the culture—art, economics, sports, vocations. Yet there are always the evil distortions of those good structures—pornography, greed, workaholism, idolatry. The Christian should identify with the good structures and seek their transformation but always separate from those evil distortions.

Second, there is no simple formula for living with or resolving this tension. Looking for *the* biblical answer to each practical question is rarely possible. Applying the principles of Scripture to each person's situation may well produce considerably different judgments. The believer's responsibility is to know God's Word, to know the mind of Christ, and then choose a course of action that most faithfully represents God's revealed will.

What are some examples of this tension? In seeking to identify with the cultural structures, while separating from their evil distortions, should a Christian own a television set, listen to non-Christian music, darn socks or throw them away? Obviously, believers will answer these questions differently, but how each is answered represents the variety of expressions within the Christian church. How Christians personally resolve this tension should produce a healthy biblical tolerance, a thankfulness for the multiplicity of expressions of Christianity. It is not easy to resolve the tension between identifying with the culture's institutions and structures and separating from the distortions of each. Some Christians will choose not to own a television, not to listen to secular music, and to discard old socks rather than darn them. Agreeing to disagree on such matters guards against unhealthy legalism and promotes a healthy dialogue about living within a non-Christian culture.

Christians must always reconcile the tension of identifying with cultural institutions, seeking to separate from culture's evil distortions, all the while seeking culture's transformation. How we live with that tension is a mark of spiritual maturity.

FOR FURTHER DISCUSSION

1. Summarize the Bible's teaching about the world and the Christian's relation to it.
2. Define the essence of each of the following models of Christians relating to culture. Give the biblical justification for each as well.
   • The separational model
   • The identificational model
   • The transformational model
3. Summarize the strengths and weaknesses of each model.
4. Robert Webber suggests a synthesis of all three models, which he calls the incarnational model. Explain what he means.
5. What does the author mean when he discusses the tension between identifying with culture's institutions and structures and yet separating from its evil distortions? What are some of the guiding principles he offers to help resolve the tension?

4

Abortion

THE ABORTION CRISIS in American civilization has been called a modern holocaust. An exaggeration? Not if you maintain a biblical view of life. The purpose of this chapter is to review briefly the history of abortion in America, lay out a biblical view of life, and answer several salient questions.

THE HISTORY OF ABORTION IN AMERICA

By a seven-to-two decision in 1973 the United States Supreme Court, in the case *Roe v. Wade*, handed down one of its most radical decisions in modern history. Generally, when a case reaches the Supreme Court, the Court is asked to rule on a constitutional question. The Court decides what the Constitution says, and in this case the Court was asked whether states (in this case Texas) can restrict a woman's right to abortion. The Court could not cite any specific part of the Constitution that established the right of abortion; nor could they find such a right in the Bill of Rights (the first ten amendments to the Constitution). Therefore, the Court set a precedent that did not appeal directly to the Constitution; instead, it declared that there is an implied right of privacy in the Constitution and on that basis established the right of women to have an abortion.

In its decision, the Court stipulated that abortions could occur up to the point of "viability" (when a child could live outside the womb) but did not define when this was. The Court further stipulated that the health of the mother must play a role in defining viability but did not define the "health of the mother" concept. The result is that the United States now has one of the most liberal abortion laws in the world. For all practical purposes, it is abortion on demand—abortion as a form of birth control. Whatever the specifics of the pregnancy, if a woman can find a sympathetic doctor or clinic, abortion is guaranteed.

The Court argued that the weight of history was on the side of abortion. The idea that life begins at conception is a modern idea and must be rejected, it contended. Why? Because there is no consensus in the medical community or among theologians or philosophers as to when life begins, the Court would not decide the issue either. The weight of the Court's argument really rested on the proposition that the unviable fetus derives its meaningfulness solely from the mother's desire to give birth to her baby. In other words, the mother's rights are established absolutely to the total exclusion of the baby's.

Today American society tolerates several types of abortion:

• Therapeutic abortion—when the termination of a pregnancy is necessary for the sake of the mother's health

• Psychiatric abortion—for the sake of the mother's mental health

• Eugenic abortion—to prevent the birth of deformed, retarded children

• Social abortion—for economic reasons, especially as related to the financial needs of the family

• Ethical abortion—in the cases of rape or incest

Again, the result is a society where abortion on demand is available to anyone desiring it.

Although gruesome, it is important to review the methods of abortion practiced in America. Each method results in the death of a living human being:

• The dilation and curettage method (D and C)—Performed early in pregnancy, the surgeon cuts the fetus and the placenta into pieces, and they are removed from the womb.

• The suction method—The surgeon draws the fetus out of the womb via a powerful suction tube, killing the baby.

• The saline method—During the latter weeks of the pregnancy, the surgeon injects a salt solution through the abdomen of the mother, poisoning the baby in about an hour. Twenty-four hours later the baby is delivered stillborn.

• Chemical abortions—This is a more recent development, usually involving the administration of a drug (e.g., RU486) to the mother that in effect causes the woman's body to abort a recently fertilized egg. This is the most problematic of methods because it does not involve a medical procedure, only the administration of a pill. There are major side effects, but this approach is probably where research on abortion methodology is headed.

• Partial-birth abortion—This term "means an abortion in which the person performing the abortion partially vaginally delivers a living fetus before killing the fetus and completing the delivery."[1]

A Biblical View of Prenatal Life

In 1973 the Supreme Court was right: There is no consensus in the culture about when life begins. God's revelation in the Bible, however, has spoken to this issue. A thorough examination of His Word reveals that God views life in the womb as of infinite value and in need of protection. The challenge is that people in most areas of the culture—law, politics, and even religion—refuse to heed God's clear teaching on this issue.

A cluster of verses in the Bible clearly establish God's view of prenatal life:

• Exodus 21:22-24—"If men struggle with each other and strike a woman with child so that she has a miscarriage . . . he shall surely be fined as the woman's husband may demand. . . . But if there is any further injury, then you shall appoint as a penalty life for life, eye for eye, tooth for tooth, hand for hand, foot for foot."

Whatever these difficult verses mean exactly, God views life in the womb as of great value. Whether by accident or by intent, to cause a woman to miscarry demands accountability on the part of the one who caused it. The Law did not treat the fetus frivolously.

• Isaiah 49:1, 5—"The LORD called Me from the womb; from the body of My mother He named Me. . . . the LORD, who formed Me from the womb to be His Servant."

Referring to Messiah, God called Him for His mission *from the womb*. Prenatal life is precious to God.

• Jeremiah 1:5—"Before I formed you in the womb I knew you, and before you were born I consecrated you."

• Luke 1:15—"[H]e will be filled with the Holy Spirit while yet in his mother's womb." As with Isaiah, God viewed Jeremiah and John the Baptist from the womb as of infinite value. He even filled John with the Holy Spirit when he was in Elizabeth's womb.

No other passage deals with the question of prenatal life so powerfully and conclusively as Psalm 139. In this wonderful psalm, David reviews four phenomenal attributes of God—His omniscience, His omnipresence, His omnipotence, and His holiness. In reviewing God's omnipotence, David reviews God's power in creating life, which he expresses as God weaving him in his mother's womb. God made his "frame," his skeleton. Then, in verse 16, he writes, "Thine eyes have seen my unformed substance. . . ." Undoubtedly, David is referring to the embryo. If correct, then the divine perspective on life is that it begins at conception. So awesome is God's omniscience and His omnipotence that He knew all about David even when he was an embryo! This is God's view of prenatal life. Therefore, abortion brings God's judgment.

ETHICAL QUESTIONS RELATING TO ABORTION

1. *Is the fetus a human being?* At conception, all aspects of human-ness, as defined by DNA, are present. Genetically, it is quite difficult to argue otherwise.

2. *Is the human fetus a person?* This is a question increasingly pressed today. The biological term *life* has been exchanged for the legal term *person.* This is a critical switch because only persons have rights, including the right to life. Paul and John Feinberg argue in their book that at conception the DNA strands of the embryo are species-specific. Furthermore, although the fetus is dependent upon the mother, he or she is an independent individual. Also, there is substantial identity between the embryo, the viable fetus, the infant, the child, the adult, and the elderly person.[2] The fetus is a person.

3. *How do the rights of the fetus relate to the rights of the mother?* American culture has so totally focused on the rights of the mother that it gives no thought to the rights of the fetus. As this chapter has shown, this is wrong. There must be a balance of rights. Somehow Christians must make the case for protecting the rights of the unborn child. Paul and John Feinberg have suggested a starting point:

> While it is difficult, and perhaps impossible, to convince a pro-abor-tionist of the personhood of the fetus, nevertheless from a purely ethical point of view it still makes sense to demand that human life should not be arbitrarily terminated, particularly when less dramatic solutions exist. Such solutions should be sought on the side of both the fetus and the mother. Having once been conceived, the fetus has no choice but to grow, just as it had no choice in its conception or its blond hair or blue eyes. Hence, the fetus is without recourse or remedy. The same is not true of the mother, who has at least three alternatives other than abortion. She can exercise initial will power by abstinence, which is grossly out of fashion today. She has the

option to use contraceptives to prevent the unwanted child. And finally, given the birth of the child, the mother can allow the living but unwanted infant to be put up for adoption.[3]

Abortion is, therefore, an unacceptable practice from God's viewpoint. He views prenatal life as of infinite worth and value. To wantonly destroy it is to destroy what He views as precious. American society may have the legal right to enforce abortion (following *Roe v. Wade*), but it does not have the ethical right before God to do so. Is it a modern holocaust? With approximately 4,000 abortions every day of every year[4] since 1973, it is difficult to argue otherwise. Multiply it out. That's 1,460,000 human babies killed per year. By the thirty-year anniversary of *Roe v. Wade* in 2003, approximately forty-three million children had been exterminated.

FOR FURTHER DISCUSSION

1. Summarize the Supreme Court's legal argument in the 1973 *Roe v. Wade* decision. In your opinion, what did the Court ignore? How would you critique their decision?
2. What types of abortion are recognized in our culture today?
3. Why might pills like RU486 be potentially problematic for those who are against abortion? Go to your local library and find information on how safe this pill really is.
4. Using the verses cited in this chapter, write a biblical position paper on why abortion is not in God's will. Be sure to stress Psalm 139.
5. Is the fetus a human? A person? How would you present an argument that the fetus is of great value and should be protected by American law? How would you make an argument that life begins at conception?

5

Euthanasia

LIKE ABORTION, euthanasia is one of the critical life issues facing American culture. With the baby boomers getting older, the pressure for widespread euthanasia will grow. In a very famous speech in the 1980s, former governor of Colorado Richard Lamb argued that the elderly must die, embracing euthanasia, to make way for the young, who simply cannot afford the medical care needed by elderly people. With the population living longer and with medical costs rising, the pressure for euthanasia as a solution over the next several decades will be relentless. How should Christians view mercy killings, doctor-assisted suicide, and "death with dignity"? One's attitude toward abortion often gives a hint of the attitude toward euthanasia because both focus on the view of human life. Whether that life is in a mother's womb or on a deathbed at age ninety, both are of infinite value to God; both bear His image.

EUTHANASIA DEFINED

The term *euthanasia* is derived from two Greek words meaning "well" or "good" death. It is today associated with language that seeks to sanitize the reality of death. "Death with dignity" focuses on constitutionally establishing the right of humans to die in a manner they choose. Usually, the reference point is old age when the bodily systems are beginning to shut down. *Mercy killing* refers to taking a person's life or allowing someone to take his or her own life to end the suffering that goes with a particular disease or a specific physical ailment or condition.

Euthanasia involves several types or methods utilized to effect the death. *Voluntary* or *involuntary euthanasia* defines whether the patient requests or has taken an active role in deciding upon the death. *Active* or *passive euthanasia* determines the method used to bring about the death. Passive euthanasia would involve, for example, allowing natural means of the body to bring death without any intervention. Not hooking a patient up to a ventilator or a heart machine would be examples because death would most certainly follow. Active euthanasia focuses on a loved one actively taking the person's life with a weapon or removing the life-sustaining equipment from the patient, bringing on death. *Direct* or *indirect euthanasia* stresses the role of the patient who dies from a specific action. Doctor-assisted suicide, where a medical doctor gives a patient the equipment or medicine to end life, would be an example of direct euthanasia. Dr. Jack Kevorkian of Michigan promotes this type of euthanasia. All types are currently practiced and growing in frequency.

A CHRISTIAN VIEW OF DEATH AND LIFE

A believer in Jesus Christ views death quite differently from an unbeliever. Death in Scripture is clearly the judgment of God upon sin. God told Adam that if he ate of the tree in the garden, he would die. When he and Eve ate, they both experienced the separation from God that resulted from sin and brought eventual physical death (Gen. 2 and 3). Sin gains authority over humans, therefore, and results in separation from God—death.

The death, burial, and resurrection of Jesus Christ dealt the deathblow to sin and defeated death in the believer's life. Because Jesus conquered death through His resurrection, the believer need not fear death. Although that person may die physically (the soul separated from the body), the separation is not permanent because of the promised resurrection. Hence, Paul can write in 1 Corinthians 15:54-55, "Death is swallowed up in victory. O death, where is your victory? O death, where is your sting?"

The believer in Jesus Christ should face death with tension. Paul gives us a window into this tension when he writes, "For to me, to live is Christ, and to die is gain" (Phil. 1:21). Death means to be with Jesus and to have all the daily struggles, both physical and spiritual, over. Although inexplicable, death is the door Christians go through to be with Christ. There is no other way, barring Christ's return for His church, for the believer to be with Christ. There is, therefore, the constant pull of heaven matched by the constant pull to remain and serve the Lord on earth. Death remains in the sovereign hand of God.

At the same time, the Bible teaches that every person, believer and unbeliever, is inherently dignified and worthy of respect. It is always proper and ethically right to fight for life. That is because men and women are created in the image and likeness of God (Gen. 1:26-27). Human life is sacred (Gen. 9:1-6), and no one should be demeaned or cursed (James 3:9-10). To treat a human, who bears God's image, as someone without dignity, to wantonly destroy life, or to assume the position of authority over the life and death of another human is to step outside of God's revelation. The Bible affirms the intrinsic worth and equal value of every human life regardless of its stage or condition. In a word, this is the Judeo-Christian view of life.

What are some implications of this high view of life? First, it seems logical since life is so valuable that it should be terminated only under highly unusual considerations. In the Netherlands, for example, the Parliament there has empowered doctors to help individuals commit suicide if they are suffering from terminal illnesses and even if they are struggling with certain emotional/mental disorders. Dr. Jack Kevorkian, now in prison, has helped more than 100 people commit suicide, some of whom were suffering from clinical depression. Such practices violate Scripture, cheapen life, and treat a human as of little value and with no dignity. In short, to allow widespread euthanasia is to foster a culture of death.

Another implication of the Judeo-Christian view of life is that personhood is defined in biological terms. As defended in the previous chapter, a human is a person whose life begins at conception, not at birth. Personhood is not defined according to I.Q., a sense of the future, a capacity to relate to other humans, or any other such criteria (more about these criteria later). The point is that God creates the life, defines its beginning as conception, and sustains the life. Humans who believe His Word will maintain the same view and always fight for life. To end life in a premeditated manner, as does Dr. Kevorkian or as is legitimized in doctor-assisted suicide, violates the Bible's high view of life.

THE QUALITY OF LIFE ETHIC

Over the last several decades in Western civilization, especially in medicine but through the entire culture, a new ethic is replacing the Judeo-Christian ethic—the quality of life ethic. At its vital center, this new ethic places relative, rather than absolute, value on human beings. Let me cite several examples:

• Joseph Fletcher argues that infanticide (killing of infants) and euthanasia are acceptable because human beings have a moral obligation to increase well-being wherever possible. "All rights are imperfect," he claims, "and can be set aside if human need requires it." Fletcher is a utilitarian who believes that objective moral norms are irrelevant in determining right and wrong. Only what brings the greatest good to the greatest number is right. He goes on: "Human happiness and well-being are the highest good . . . and . . . therefore any ends or purposes which that ideal or standard validates are just, right, good." Suicide and mercy killing are acceptable to Fletcher because "a morally good end can justify a relatively bad means."[1]

• For Joseph Fletcher, to meet the criteria of being truly human, a person must possess minimal intelligence, a sense of the future and the past, a capacity to relate to others, and a balance between rationality and feelings. For example, a human with an I.Q. of 40 is questionably a person; one with an I.Q. of 20 or below is definitely not a person. Following Fletcher's logic, an infant, an adult, or an elderly person with a degenerative brain disease would not meet these criteria and thus would forfeit the right to life.

• Michael Tooley, a philosopher, formerly at Stanford and now at the University of Colorado, thinks it unfortunate that most people use terms like "person" and "human being" interchangeably. Persons have rights, but not every human being can properly be regarded as a person, Tooley believes. His rule: An organism has a serious right to life only if it possesses the concept of a self as a continuing subject of experiences and other mental states and believes itself to be a continuing entity. For Tooley, infanticide is allowable up to a week after birth. Presumably, an elderly person with a degenerative brain disease would also not meet his criteria and thus would forfeit the right to life.[2]

This new quality of life ethic is frightening. Rejecting any claim to ethical absolutes, this system embraces subjective criteria to define life's value and ends up justifying both euthanasia and infanticide. It violates all aspects of life's value as defined by the image of God concept and places humans in the seat of the sovereign God. Using subjective criteria, the quality of life ethic empowers other humans to decide who lives and who dies.

ANOTHER ALTERNATIVE—THE CHRISTIAN HOSPICE

This chapter has rejected the propensity of the present culture to redefine personhood and justify euthanasia. However, what does a Christian do when a loved one is diagnosed with a terminal disease? What does one do if someone dear develops Alzheimer's disease or Huntington's disease? What if extremely painful cancer develops, and the only outlook is months or years of pain to be followed by death?

There is no easy answer, but the Christian hospice movement is offering a powerful alternative for Christians today. Sometimes care is provided for dying patients within a nursing home facility or their own home. It involves managing pain with drugs, giving loving comfort, and providing daily service to meet all human needs, whatever the specific situation. The care is complemented by spiritual encouragement from God's Word, mixed with prayer and edifying opportunities as reminders of God's goodness and of eternal life. Death is not easy, but, as mentioned earlier in this chapter, the Christian approaches death differently than the unbeliever. The loving, empathetic, nail-scarred hands of Jesus are outstretched to welcome His child home to heaven. Hospice care provides the dignified alternative to honor God's creation (life) all the while preparing the dying saints for the promise that awaits them. It preserves the dignity of life that the mercy killers promise but cannot deliver.

FOR FURTHER DISCUSSION

1. What does the term *euthanasia* mean? Define its various types.
   - Voluntary versus involuntary
   - Active versus passive
   - Direct versus indirect
   - Death with dignity
   - Mercy killing
2. Summarize the Judeo-Christian view of life and describe how this view relates to the debate over euthanasia. Also summarize how a Christian views death.
3. What is the quality of life ethic? How does it differ from the Judeo-Christian view?
4. How does the Christian hospice movement provide a biblical alternative to current practices of euthanasia? Research your own community for hospice care services.

6

Bioethics

NO AREA OF CULTURE is advancing faster than biotechnology and genetics technology. So serious is this development that government, in writing legislation, is screaming for guidelines and advice on how to deal with these explosive issues. For example, in 1997 Governor Ben Nelson of Nebraska asked me to serve on the Human Genetics Technology Commission for the state of Nebraska. Chartered for one year, the commission's charge was to write a report giving guidelines and recommendations in the complex area of human genetics technology. The federal government, for example, funded the Human Genome Project, which mapped the DNA strands to identify every human gene and its function. The results, announced in April 2003, mean a degree of control that the human race has never had before. What will we do with this knowledge and this control?

To further illustrate the importance of thinking biblically about this matter of biotechnology, consider the following situations and ponder how you would respond:

• Suppose a Christian couple whom you knew well came to you for some counsel. They are infertile, and they shared with you the several options their doctor offered that might solve their infertility problem. The doctor said that the wife could be artificially inseminated using someone else's sperm. No one would ever know. The doctor likewise described a process known as *in vitro* fertilization, where several of the wife's eggs would be removed from her body, and likewise sperm would be provided by the husband. In a petri dish, the eggs would be fertilized by the sperm, and the best one(s) would be implanted back into the wife's womb.

• Suppose another couple, also struggling with infertility, sought your advice about hiring a surrogate to carry a baby produced through artificial insemination with the husband's sperm. When born, the baby would, by contract, be turned over to the couple.

• Suppose a Christian couple wants to have a child but knows that if they have a boy, he will be a hemophiliac. They know about the possibility of gender selection techniques that would insure a girl to a 95 percent probability.

• Suppose you have friends who are afflicted with dwarfism. They would like to have children who will grow to normal height, to prevent their children much of the pain they have suffered. They discover a procedure where a doctor can alter the genes of the fetus *in utero* (in the uterus) to insure more height.

Each one of these scenarios is either currently being done or could potentially be done. The power of medical technology is awesome but frightening, because the human race is now able to manipulate and control areas of life unknown to all previous generations. Guidance from God's Word is clearly needed.

MODERN VIEWS OF HUMANITY

Since the Enlightenment of the eighteenth century, the Western view of humans has undergone radical change. Each subsequent theorist has contributed to viewing the human being as more of a machine than an image-bearer of God. For each of the following individuals or movements, humans are no longer the crown of God's creation; instead, humans are products of impersonal forces beyond human control. The last 200 years have not been good ones for those who view humans as unique.[1]

• Charles Darwin proposed the theory of evolution in his books *Origin of Species* (1859) and *The Descent of Man* (1872). For the Darwinian hypothesis, humans are merely products of the same force of natural selection that produced all other life forms. Nothing unique about humans here.

• Sigmund Freud's various theories postulated that all human behavior is unconsciously or subconsciously motivated. In many cases these forces are remarkably powerful and deep in the subconscious. The whole discussion of sin and human accountability was changing.

• Benjamin Watson and B. F. Skinner argued that behavior is all you can really study in humans and that human behavior is totally explained by heredity or the environment. Divine purpose or control is out of the behaviorist's picture.

• Today sociologists and historians emphasize the social and historical forces that inform and explain virtually all human corporate behavior. God, theology, and human sin play little or no role in these explanations.

• Geneticists and physiologists emphasize the genetic and chemical causes of human behavior.

The result of these various perspectives is to minimize human accountability and to discover *the* explanation that covers all aspects of human behavior. An all-inclusive understanding of the forces—internal and external—that explain human behavior is the objective of each of these disciplines. A corollary is that once these forces are understood, it is possible to control human behavior, either to improve it or to eliminate aspects most harmful to the human race.

HISTORICAL DEVELOPMENTS PRODUCING AN OPENNESS TOWARD HUMAN MANIPULATION

The new openness in Western civilization to seeking to control and manipulate humans arose from several historical developments since the Enlightenment. First is a mechanistic view of human beings. For example, with organ transplants in medicine, the maintenance of organ donor banks, sperm donor banks, discussion about the harvesting of organs from cadavers, etc., it is not an immense step to view humans as mere machines. When one part breaks down, another is ready to replace it. This is not medicine's intent, but the level of expectation is that somewhere there is a "part" for me. What naturally follows is a view of the human body as a machine that with proper maintenance and repairs can keep on functioning. This view produces an openness to accepting manipulation of conception and genetics.

Another development is the increasing human control over nearly every aspect of life. We live in climate-controlled buildings, drive climate-controlled vehicles, access voluminous amounts of information worldwide at the click of a mouse, can travel anywhere in the world in less than a day, and live longer than at any time in recent human history. The reason? Technology. Because of human dependence on technology, there is the natural expectation that all human problems can ultimately be solved by technology, including infertility problems, health problems, and emotional problems.

The concept of the scientific imperative is another cause of modern technological openness. This concept assumes that because technology has made a particular procedure, invention, or practice possible, we therefore as a civilization must go forward with it. The scientist's "can" becomes the civilization's "ought." This powerful assumption is pervasive in Western civilization. Globally, the invention of deadly weapons or procedures (even something as unthinkable as chemical and biological warfare) relentlessly presses on until someone determines these weapons must be produced. The same logic drives conception techniques and genetic procedures. Once the procedure is developed, it is nearly impossible to stop someone, somewhere from using it.

Another development producing this openness toward technological manipulation is the modern emphasis on pleasure and pain reduction as virtual moral imperatives. Think of common, everyday headaches. The typical drugstore in America is filled with dozens of headache remedies. Pain and discomfort are foreign to our lifestyle, and our expectations are that there should be a pill somewhere for each ailment. This expectation transfers as well to the "good life" that modern conveniences have produced. We expect, almost demand ease, comfort, and daily pleasure in the forms of good food, entertainment, and self-indulgence. In the words of Francis Schaeffer, "personal peace and affluence" drive Western civilization.[2] The result is an openness toward and the positive expectation about technological manipulation of human beings.

The doctrine of the autonomous self is the final development that has fostered this technological openness. *Autonomous* means "self-law." With the current view of law and with the pervasive practice of defending human behavior in terms of rights and liberties (e.g., abortion, euthanasia, homosexuality), individualism has been heightened to an extreme level. Western civilization has accepted the proposition that the individual is nearly sovereign in his or her thinking and behavior. This view is epitomized in the 1992 *Casey* case, which stated that "at the heart of liberty is the right of every individual to decide his or her own meaning of the universe. . . ."[3] Issues of control and manipulation of genes or of conception are in the hands of the individual.

TYPES OF HUMAN MANIPULATION

In the scenarios mentioned to introduce this chapter, several examples of genetic and conception manipulation were cited, namely *in vitro* fertilization, artificial insemination using donor sperm (AID), surrogate motherhood, gender selection, and genetic surgery *in utero*. In addition dozens of other technological procedures are possible or are now being discussed:

• *Cloning*—A variety of methods are currently being used in animal research, but the core idea is to remove the DNA material of a cell's nucleus from one creature (e.g., a sheep) and place that material into the nucleus of a sheep embryo's cell, eventually producing a virtual duplicate of the original. Technologically, this procedure could be done with humans, but social resistance to such a procedure remains strong. It is probable that cloning will gradually become acceptable.

• *Human/animal organ transplantation*—For decades medicine has used animal parts to cure human sickness. Cow veins have been stitched into the arms of humans needing dialysis treatment for kidney disease. Valves from pigs have been utilized to mend faulty human hearts as well. But in recent years, doctors at Loma Linda Medical Center in California have replaced a sickly child's heart with a baboon's heart. Animal livers have been used in other children's bodies. Discussion of using other animal organs to deal with children's diseases goes on.

• *A variation on the* in vitro *fertilization theme*—In vitro fertilization is producing legal challenges as, for example, in divorces where the former spouses battle over who actually has authority over the fertilized eggs.

The issue of frozen embryos grows more complex both legally and ethically as the practice grows. The United Kingdom has a law that frozen embryos cannot be kept for longer than five years. In 1997 over 3,000 frozen embryos were nearing the five-year threshold and faced destruction. The Vatican condemned the imminent destruction; couples and organizations from all over the world offered to "adopt" the embryos. They were destroyed. We do not know how to deal with these situations.

In Australia a couple had previously frozen several embryos produced through *in vitro* fertilization, but were tragically killed in a car accident. The legal authorities were struggling to determine whether the embryos would be legally able to inherit their parents' estate. Again there were no legal parameters.

• *Genetic testing*—Suppose that researchers are successful in using the data generated by the Human Genome Project to discover the relation of every human gene to all major diseases. Suppose also that widespread genetic testing occurs and the knowledge of each citizen's genetic makeup is available. Will insurance companies then refuse to insure people found to have faulty genes, under the standard of a "pre-existing condition"?

Although bizarre and in some cases extreme, these scenarios represent just a sampling of the legal, medical, and ethical morass reproductive and genetic technology has produced. We not only have a crisis of moral authority, having no absolute framework for addressing these issues, but law and insurance have not caught up with medicine. There is a crying need for some guidelines.

GUIDING PRINCIPLES FOR CONCEPTION AND GENETIC PRACTICES

A list of guiding principles follows for consideration in dealing with issues of genetic and reproductive manipulation. This is probably not an exhaustive list. Its goal is to offer some guidance rooted in or inferred from God's Word. These guiding principles do not provide answers to all the issues raised in this chapter; nor do they mean that all reproductive and genetic research should be halted or outlawed. Rather, they should guide Christians into making wise decisions in these excruciatingly difficult areas of modern life.

1. *Human beings are created in God's image.* This makes humans more valuable than any other of God's creatures. We can then stipulate that humans are always more valuable (intrinsically so) than all other created things. There is an essential creation-order distinction between humans and other created things (both living and nonliving). The material in Genesis 1 and 2 establishes these guidelines.

2. *Issues and practices in both reproduction and genetics fall under the stewardship responsibility of humans.* In Genesis 1:26ff., God creates humans—male and female—in His image and then gives them the responsibility to "be fruitful and multiply, and fill the earth, and subdue it; and rule over the fish of the sea and over the birds of the sky, and over every living thing that moves on the earth" (1:28). Verse 29 extends this dominion to plants, trees, and seeds. Although colored by the reality of human sin, this dominion status is repeated for Noah in Genesis 9:1-2. Because God is sovereign and humans have dominion status, accountability of the human is a necessary corollary. This matter of accountability has powerful implications in the areas of reproductive and genetic manipulation. These technologies give humans

power never realized before in history. Because humans are cursed with sin, it is difficult to be optimistic about the ultimate use of some of the genetic technologies. What must penetrate the human mind in this technology is that God is sovereign; we are stewards!

3. *The question of using these technologies is probably not so much whether to use them but how, when, and at what cost.* For example, *in vitro* fertilization involves multiple embryos produced in a petri dish. One or two embryos are implanted in the woman's womb. The remaining embryos are either destroyed or frozen. If life begins at conception (as the Bible infers), then destruction of the embryos is the destruction of life. Gender selection of children, which is now possible, could seriously upset the gender balance of any civilization. Empowering parents to exercise this kind of control seems unwise, even foolish. The challenges of human cloning are so immense that proceeding with caution does not even seem wise; outright prohibition seems necessary. In many of these technologies, we simply do not know the effects of their widespread use.

4. *Human life itself is of higher value than the quality of human life.* With the eternal perspective that the Bible gives, many of these technologies border on the quality of human life ethic. Consider the example of the very short couple at the chapter's beginning. Exodus 4:11 contains God's response to Moses' claim that he lacked eloquence: "Who has made man's mouth? Or who makes him dumb or deaf, or seeing or blind? Is it not I, the LORD?" God's sovereignty extends to matters of stature. That God created this couple in His image establishes value—not height, or sight, or hearing. The same question can be raised about controlling the color of eyes, hair, or gender of a baby still *in utero*. Where might such practices, seemingly innocuous at first, end? What might the ungodly do with such power and control?

5. *From God's perspective, concern for the improvement of the "inner person" is always more important than concern for improvement of the "outer person."* Because of the inevitability of death, no procedure or practice will prevent it. Perhaps that is why Scripture gives focus to such issues as the fruit of the Spirit (Gal. 5:22-23) and the eight quality traits listed in the Beatitudes (Matt. 5:1-16). In the Bible's perspective these seem more important than using certain technologies with a goal that approaches human perfectibility. Carl Henry argued that there is clear biblical warrant for procedures that restore people; there is no clear biblical warrant for manipulation toward perfection, an insightful guideline in approaching some of the technologies discussed in this chapter.[4]

6. *When one views God's creation, one realizes that values like unpredictability, variety, diversity, and uniqueness are central to God's creative work.* Some of the genetic technologies seem, at least potentially, to violate His values. Control over gender selection and other human features could produce a "sameness" that God did not intend. Do people know how to exercise wisely the kind of power and control these procedures bring? With the reality of sin ever before us, it is difficult to answer in the affirmative. Caution—methodical, meticulous caution—is needed in approaching the genetic minefield. That is why the prudent biblical stance is that if a procedure will likely and eventually violate biblical guidelines, it is best to proceed on a very selective basis or to not proceed at all.

7. *Finally, this civilization must critically examine the scientific imperative.* Simply because society can pursue a particular medical, reproductive, or genetic procedure does not mandate that it must! Especially in the area of genetics, "can" does not mandate "ought." The potential for power and control and its obvious abuse mandates an examination of this imperative. Perhaps with some of these procedures, it would be wise not to do them at all.[5]

This chapter has introduced you to issues fraught with complexity and uncertainty. We simply do not know where all of this will end. Therefore guidelines, inferred from God's Word, are imperative for analysis.

FOR FURTHER DISCUSSION

1. Review the role each of the following played in redefining humans and their uniqueness in Western civilization:
   • Darwin
   • Freud
   • Watson and Skinner
2. Summarize four or five developments in Western civilization that produced an openness toward manipulation of conception and genetics.
3. Summarizing some of the procedures discussed in the chapter, which ones would you approve or disapprove if Carl Henry's dictum (restore rather than manipulate) was followed?
4. Discuss the scientific imperative. Is it valid or not? Explain.
5. List and summarize five of the guiding principles discussed at the end of the chapter.

7

Human Sexuality

THE DOCTRINE OF the autonomous self, mentioned in chapter 6, with its demand for rights and liberties, has resulted in a redefining of human sexuality in Western civilization. What only a few decades ago was unthinkable, gradually became debatable and is now becoming acceptable. The desire to legitimize the homosexual lifestyle is clearly part of a strategy to make it acceptable. That strategy is working. In politics, business, television and other entertainment, and the arts, the homosexual lifestyle is commonly presented as an alternate way of life. How should we think about this? As part of the "culture wars" ravaging society, is this an issue of moral authority? This book argues yes. Our goal is to focus on what God has said about the issue and then construct a strategy to impact culture on this matter.

THE BIBLE AND HUMAN SEXUALITY

When discussing homosexuality, evangelicals usually point to the Levitical code, to Sodom and Gomorrah, or to Paul's statements in the New Testament. I believe this is an error. The proper place to begin thinking about this issue is Genesis 2. After giving clear instructions to Adam about his stewardship of the Garden, God concludes that it is not good that Adam be alone (v. 18). To prove this to Adam, God brings all the animals before him to name (vv. 19-20). Although this act establishes his authority over the animals, it also serves as an object lesson for Adam. He is the only creature of God truly alone. So God creates the woman as his complement, his helper (vv. 21-23).

Moses then offers a theological commentary on what God did with Adam and Eve (vv. 24-25). First, God established the paradigm for marriage. The man is to leave his family with the conscious understanding that he is establishing a new family unit. Second, that means "to cleave" (like glue) to his wife. Third, in separating from his family of origin and making the unqualified commitment to his wife, the two will "become one flesh." This concept does symbolize the sexual intercourse that physically unites the two human beings, but it also symbolizes the merging of two personalities, male and female, into a complementary whole. Their personalities, their idiosyncrasies, and their uniqueness do not cease. Instead, these two totally different human beings merge into a perfect complement where both—now together—serve God in their integrity.[1]

In verse 25, Moses further comments that this couple is "naked" and not "ashamed." They were so totally centered on each other that they did not think of self. We can properly infer that their sexual oneness was characterized by no shame or discomfort either. Their physical love was beautiful and fulfilling; no selfish or carnal lust was present. The wonder of romantic love was perfectly present in this first marriage.

Theologically, what do we learn from this passage? How does this passage establish the model for a proper understanding of human sexuality and marriage? Allow me to suggest several lessons:

• When Jesus and Paul deal with questions of marriage or human sexuality, they always refer back to this creation ordinance of Genesis 2:18-25 (Matt. 19:1-12; Mark 10:1-12; 1 Cor. 7:10-11). What is stated in these verses transcends culture and time. They constitute God's ideal for sexuality and marriage.

• Marriage is to be monogamous and heterosexual—the standard, the ideal, for all marriages. From this passage it is impossible to justify polygamy or homosexuality. "Same-sex" marriages are not an option. With this standard established for marriage in the creation ordinance, the other scriptural passages dealing with human sexuality are all measured against Genesis 2. Each maintains that fornication, adultery, or homosexuality is an aberration, a radical departure from God's clear standard.

• Genesis 19:1-11 is the story of Sodom, which God utterly destroyed with fire. Homosexual commentators see the sin of the men as a violation of the ancient Near Eastern hospitality codes. But verse 5 and Lot's response in verse 8 demonstrate unequivocally that these men were intent on homosexual relations. Their behavior was a deliberate departure from God's clear revelation in Genesis 2.

• In Leviticus 18:22, 29 and 20:13, homosexual commentators often argue that we set aside most other parts of the Levitical law; so why emphasize this one so adamantly? Although Jesus' finished work on Calvary's cross did render inoperative much of the Levitical law and practices (the argument of Hebrews), issues of human sexuality transcend the law because of the creation ordinance of God in Genesis 2. What God says in Leviticus 18 and 20 is tied clearly to His standard established at creation. Homosexuality is ethically wrong.

• Paul's argument in Romans 1:26-27 about the debased sexual practices cited in the verses hangs on his use of the word *natural*. Homosexual commentators argue that Paul is condemning unfaithfulness in the homosexual relationship, not homosexuality itself. However, *natural* and *unnatural* can only be understood as departure or adherence to some standard that determines what natural and unnatural is. That standard can only be the one established in God's creation ordinance in Genesis 2.

• To motivate the Corinthians out of their spiritual complacency, Paul lists in 1 Corinthians 6:9 the various categories of sinners God will keep out of His kingdom. His goal is that they will examine themselves. Among those listed are "effeminate" and "homosexuals." Paul Feinberg argues that these two Greek words focus on both the active and the passive partner in the homosexual relationship. The emphasis of the passage is not on unfaithfulness to the homosexual partner, as the homosexual commentators contend, but on the very homosexual act itself.[2]

• In 1 Timothy 1:10, Paul also condemns homosexuality as contrary to "sound teaching." The issue is not unfaithfulness to a homosexual partner. The issue is engaging in something that violates God's clearly revealed standard. In this case, "sound teaching" is God's revelation in His creation ordinance, just as "liars," "kidnappers," "perjurers," and others would violate His standards revealed elsewhere (the Ten Commandments, for example).

In summary, the Bible resoundingly condemns the homosexual lifestyle as contrary to the ethical standard God established in His creation ordinance of marriage. Without some benchmark to settle the ethical debate on human sexuality, there will continually be heated confrontations within the culture. God's Word provides that benchmark; the human response of obedience is the only acceptable option.

CAUSATION—GENETIC OR ENVIRONMENTAL?

There is a great debate ensuing among psychologists and scholars over the causation of homosexuality. Is it genetically determined, or is it environmental? Those in the gay community argue passionately that being gay is genetically determined. Those who are in the religious gay community say that this is God's gift, claiming sexual orientation is created by God, and there is nothing anyone can do about it. Simon LaVay, himself a homosexual, has done tests on cadavers who were homosexual and has found that the pituitary gland of these homosexual men is larger than that of non-homosexual men. Jeffrey Satinover presents compelling evidence that questions LaVay's research and the research and data of all claims that homosexuality is a genetic issue.[3]

Satinover's conclusions show that homosexuality is a learned way of life produced by circumstances that result in the choice of homosexuality. This is not a popular position today, especially in many universities and even among those of the American Psychiatric Association, which used to see homosexuality as a pathology in need of treatment. Satinover shows that the reason this organization altered its position was not due to science but to politics.[4]

At this point in time, there is no consensus on settling this question. Satinover's book is a powerful indictment of the politically correct agenda driving so many professional organizations, as well as the national gay movement itself. Gays seek legitimacy, and "fudging" evidence and research can often be a way to achieve it. Other serious researchers, some of whom are evangelical Christians, still argue for some kind of genetic role in the causation of homosexuality.[5] One important point to remember is that even if there is a genetic role in homosexuality's causation, the Bible still condemns it, and God's power is sufficient to overcome it, no matter what its cause.

HOMOSEXUALITY AND THE CHURCH

Over the last decades, the homosexual issue has deeply impacted the church of Jesus Christ. A brief review of some of the salient issues demonstrates how complex the issue has become. Let me list a few developments:

• The Metropolitan Community Church movement is spreading throughout the United States. Claiming to be evangelical, this "denomination" reads and teaches from the Bible and defends the homosexual lifestyle as completely biblical. I summarized some of its views on the human sexuality passages earlier in this chapter. A similar group is Evangelicals Concerned, centered in New York City.

• Most mainline denominations are struggling over the issue of whether to ordain practicing homosexuals into the ministry. The question is totally divisive in many of these denominations, potentially splitting some if it is not resolved. Others are struggling with the matter of same-sex marriages. Should denominational pastors perform such ceremonies? Denominations are deeply divided over this question.

• Two "evangelicals," Letha Scanzoni and Virginia Mollenkott, in 1978 published a book that shook the evangelical world, *Is the Homosexual My Neighbor?*—to which they answered yes![6]

The issues of homosexuality are massive, having tentacles that reach wide. But the bottom-line issue remains what has God said. This chapter has argued that the creation ordinance of God leaves no room for the homosexual lifestyle. It is a sin and must be faced as such.

CONFRONTING AND DISCIPLING THE HOMOSEXUAL

In 1985 Don Baker published a book, *Beyond Rejection*, which chronicles the story of Jerry, who struggled with homosexuality from his childhood, through seminary, and into marriage. It provides a needed window into the extreme difficulties of this struggle and yet the hope provided by Jesus Christ. Based on the balance brought by this book, let me suggest several action points for dealing with the reality of homosexuality in our culture:[7]

• *Remember that to the homosexual subculture, evangelicals are the enemy!* Because the Bible speaks so clearly on this issue, and evangelicals reflect that truth, there is no room for compromise or discussion. Patience, love, and compassion are needed as relationships are developed.

• *Remember that homosexuality is a sin.* That is the point of the earlier part of this chapter. But, although scandalous, it is not the "worst" sin. God's grace is completely sufficient to deal with this bondage.

• *Unconditional love is an absolute requirement in ministry to those in bondage to this sin.* Compassion, empathy, patience, and commitment for the long haul are necessary prerequisites. The reality is that many will fall back into the lifestyle, even after conversion to Jesus Christ. That is why organizations like Exodus International are so critical.[8] A ready-made support group of encouragers and accountability are central to this organization's ministry.

• *Repentance must always be the goal.* There must be a complete break with the past and with the lifestyle. No compromise or middle ground is available. Here again Exodus International insists on a crucial requirement for ministering to the homosexual.

There is no sign that the homosexual issue will subside in the culture war raging in Western civilization. Somehow the church of Jesus Christ must be able with one hand to declare that this lifestyle is morally and ethically wrong, while with the other reaching out the hand of love, acceptance, and compassion. Only God, working through His Spirit to enable the church, can accomplish this most difficult and seemingly impossible task.

FOR FURTHER DISCUSSION

1. What does the author mean by the creation ordinance on human sexuality? How do the following passages relate to it:
   • Genesis 19:1-11
   • Leviticus 18:22, 29; 20:13
   • Romans 1:26-27
   • 1 Corinthians 6:9-11
   • 1 Timothy 1:10
2. Summarize the debate between genetic versus environmental causes of homosexuality. Which do you find most compelling?
3. Summarize how this ethical issue impacts the church. Investigate your own church's official position, especially if you come from a mainline denominational church.
4. What attitude should Christians have toward homosexuals? If one of your children believed he or she is a homosexual, how would you respond? How should this issue be handled?
5. Does this issue suggest anything about the importance of both male and female role models for children from an early age?

8

The Christian and Politics

SHOULD CHRISTIANS VOTE? Should they run for political office? Is it proper for Christians to engage in civil disobedience? What exactly is the ethical obligation the believer owes to the state? Does the Bible speak to any of these questions? This chapter will argue that Scripture gives clear guidelines for all of these questions, giving the Christian a framework for making an impact in the political arena for righteousness and the kingdom of God.

CHRISTIAN OBLIGATION TOWARD THE STATE

The New Testament teaches clearly that the Christian does have an obligation toward the state. This is the central point of Jesus' teaching in Mark 12:13-17, where, when questioned about paying taxes to Rome, He answers that we "render to Caesar the things that are Caesar's, and to God the things that are God's." We owe obligation obviously to God and His kingdom but also to the state because He created it, and it serves His purpose.[1] This passage makes clear that the obligation to the state stems from being a member of the state.

The apostle Paul expands on Jesus' argument in Romans 13:1-7 when he argues that the Christian is to submit to government because God established it. No ruler, president, prime minister, or tyrant has power that did not first come from God (Dan. 4:17-25). In verses 3 and 4 of Romans 13, Paul also argues that the state is to administer justice and thwart evil. This is the principal reason that God created government in the first place (Gen. 9:5-7). Paul seems to imply that this function of the state is actually conducive to the spread of the gospel.

The final reason for the Christian's obligation toward government is found in 1 Timothy 2:1-7. Here the believer is instructed to pray for those in authority in the state, in order that "we may lead a tranquil and quiet life in all godliness and dignity" (v. 2). As C. E. B. Cranfield argues from verses 3-7, "It is implied that God wills the state as a means to promoting peace and quiet among men, and that God desires such peace and quiet because they are in some way conducive to men's salvation."[2]

THE CHRISTIAN'S RESPONSIBILITY TO THE STATE

That Christians have a responsibility toward the state is clear, but what exactly is the content of that obligation?[3] First, the believer owes the state respect. Romans 13:7 and 1 Peter 2:17 both admonish the Christian to honor and respect government officials as ministers of God who have been ordained by Him and are accountable to Him for their solemn trust of promoting justice and thwarting evil. Respect involves treating with full seriousness even individuals who have no respect for the office or their high calling to that office. That dimension, therefore, necessitates administering rebuke and calling to account those rulers who abuse their office or treat the office itself with contempt. In the United States, respect would mean utilizing the constitutional means of impeachment to judge any federal official who has committed treason, bribery, or other "high crimes or misdemeanors."[4]

Second, the believer owes the state, its agents, and its duly enacted laws obedience (Titus 3:1; 1 Pet. 2:13-17; Rom. 13:1-7). Jesus paid the temple tax, and Paul apologized for speaking disrespectfully to a ruler. Further, Jesus' birth occurred in Bethlehem because Joseph was obedient to an oppressive government issuing a tax-assessing edict. Yet the New Testament mandate is neither slavish nor absolute; we see Peter and John defying the Sanhedrin's order to stop preaching. The issue apparently to them was clear: We obey the state until it is a sin to do so. Here civil disobedience was not merely permitted by God's Spirit; it was demanded (Acts 4:19ff.; 5:29). If the government commands something that God forbids or forbids something that God commands, we must disobey. That disobedience cannot involve violence or vandalism, actions that contradict prudence and civil order.

Thus, disobedience should never be taken lightly or with undue haste. Christians do have a higher law than that of human government. But God gives human governments in the main His seal of approval, and disobedience to them should be considered with great caution. Lynn

Buzzard offers seven questions the believer should ask when facing the possibility of disobedience to the state:

1. How directly and immediately does the opposed government policy contradict an unequivocal biblical teaching?

2. What is the counsel of the Christian community about this policy? Where do godly leaders rank it among threats to the faith that must be addressed? What do they say about what the faithful person's response ought to be? To what extent have alternative legal protests been exhausted?

3. What harms to society and order are likely to result from the considered act of civil disobedience, and how do these harms compare with the desired benefits?

4. Will the form of civil disobedience evidence moral consistency and further proper respect for principled law and a moral society?

5. To what extent will the "witness" be heard and understood by the public and by government authorities?

6. To what extent are the acts central to maintaining my integrity as a person? To what extent may they reflect personal frustration and anger rather than a principled response?

7. To what extent does the idea for the act of civil disobedience issue from thought sources alien to a biblical worldview? Is it based upon biblical principles about the uses of power and coercion, the witness of the cross, and the sovereignty of God, or is it based upon purely naturalistic, humanistic principles?[5]

Third, the believer must pay taxes (Mark 12:13-17; Matt. 22:15-22; Luke 20:20-26; Rom. 13:6-7). Jesus makes the payment of taxes the fundamental mark of obligation to the state, regardless of the state's morality or ethical bankruptcy. This is clear because Jesus and Paul were both writing of tax payment to the Roman Empire, a corrupt, evil, and ethically repulsive state.

Fourth, the believer must pray for those in authority (1 Tim. 2:1ff.). Such praying is an essential part of the debt owed, whether the official is pagan or Christian, religiously indifferent or antireligious, just or unjust. I am often frustrated by Christians who relentlessly criticize governmental officials but rarely, if ever, pray for those officials. God can use praying to effect righteousness in the state's laws or to bring an unbelieving government official to Jesus Christ. Constructive criticism and calling the state to accountability need to be balanced with fervent, persevering prayer.

INFERENCES FOR A CHRISTIAN LIVING IN A DEMOCRACY

These, then, are the four ethical obligations the Christian owes to the state, but out of these obligations grow certain other inferences that are especially acute for the Christian who lives in a democracy. First, the Christian should vote. In normal circumstances, according to Cranfield, failure to vote "is to abandon one's share of responsibility for the main-tenance of the state as a just state and therefore a dereliction of one's duty as a Christian."[6] Second, the Christian should keep as fully and reliably informed as possible concerning political, social, and economic issues. This necessitates diligent reading of newspapers and news magazines, careful watching of television news broadcasts, and reasoned, balanced discussion of such issues with friends and colleagues. Third is criticism of the government, its policies, and its agents in light of God's revelation. The Bible becomes the grid through which the Christian evaluates the state's actions and policies; the believer is willing to call the state to righ-teousness in light of God's Word. Finally, the Christian should work for just and righteous laws and oppose those policies and decisions that are unjust and unrighteous. In a democracy Christians would become involved in activities such as working for candidates who support jus-tice and righteousness and supporting, through calling and writing let-ters, legislation that reflects genuine biblical righteousness.

CHRISTIAN INVOLVEMENT IN GOVERNMENT AND POLITICS

Increasing involvement in politics and government has grave dangers for the Christian. To provide the maximum impact for righteousness in government, a proper and balanced perspective is needed. This neces-sitates ridding ourselves of what Chuck Colson calls a "starry-eyed view of political power."[7] Some Christians think that by marshaling a Christian voting bloc, Christ's kingdom on earth can be established. The external and limited good that political power can achieve should not be confused with the internal and infinite good that God's grace pro-duces. Further, there is danger in what Colson calls the "political illu-sion," the notion that all human problems can be solved by political institutions. This belief is idolatrous because the Bible declares that the root problem of society is spiritual. What the Christian seeks through government is justice, not power. Our goal is, therefore, to move the culture toward the righteousness of God's revelation. The job of total spiritual transformation is the role of Christ, through the church, not the state.

How then does the Christian decide what to support and what to reject in politics? How does one decide whom to support in elections? For what kinds of laws should the believer work and fight? Robert Dugan, former director of the National Association of Evangelicals, suggests five major principles to guide the Christian in assessing potential candidates and laws:

1. *The preeminence of religious liberty*—Any candidate or legislation that restricts the practice of religious faith should be resisted.

2. *The protection of life as sacred*—Candidates or legislation that treat life frivolously or that seek to destroy it (e.g., abortion, euthanasia, infanticide) should be resisted and defeated.

3. *Provision of justice for all*—Candidates and legislation must reflect God's concern for justice and equity. The book of Amos is convincing evidence that God desires government to promote laws that protect the poor and disadvantaged from exploitation and oppression.

4. *Preservation of the traditional family*—One of the clear teachings of the Bible is that the family is a critical institution to God. Legislation that negatively impacts the family should be rejected. For example, tax legislation that promotes single-parent families or penalizes a father for living with his family is counterproductive. The promotion of same-sex marriages runs counter to God's revelation and should be rejected.

5. *The promotion of Judeo-Christian values in education and legislation*—For example, values of honesty, integrity, personal responsibility, and accountability can be easily undermined by a leader who wantonly lies and shows disrespect for the law. Fraud, bribery, and corruption undermine public trust and confidence and are terribly destructive. Education must reinforce the values of parents and not undermine their authority (Deut. 6:1-10).[8]

Christians, then, as salt and light (Matt. 5:13-16), should seek to effect righteous change in the culture through the political process, not because the kingdom comes from Washington, but because God expects us to be serving and waiting (1 Thess. 1:9-10).

THE ROLE OF THE CHURCH

Should the church as a local body of believers function as a political caucus or coalition or operate at any other level of political activity?

Some Christians believe local churches should not be involved in political activities. They reason, first, that the laws of the United States are clear concerning local churches not engaging in *direct* political activities (endorsing a particular candidate). To do so would violate (and possibly result in the loss of) the nonprofit status for the organizations. Secondly, the Bible gives no mandate or even logical inference for local church political activity. Thirdly, there is no evidence of the early church being involved in politics. Furthermore, the local church often lacks the necessary expertise for reasoned political involvement and can even find its witness severely harmed. The local church is a spiritual body, rooted in God's revelation. Christians should individually be involved in the political arena, but the local church will do so to its peril.

On the other hand, some Christians believe the local church is not ordained as a political body; yet because individuals are charged with this responsibility, the collective group involvement can most certainly impact politics and government. Therefore, local churches *should be* involved with political issues relating to morality and justice.

Christians walk a careful balance between understanding the Christian obligation toward the state and seeking to influence that state for righteousness and justice. The two spheres of the Christian's life—the church and the state—must be kept in balance. Each has a divine job to do; neither should encroach upon the responsibility of the other.

FOR FURTHER DISCUSSION

1. Discuss why Mark 12:13-17 is foundational for the Christian's obligation toward the state.
2. What are three reasons the author suggests for the Christian's obligation to the state?
3. Summarize the specific political responsibility of each of these (when possible use Scripture references):
   • respect
   • obedience
   • payment of taxes
   • prayer
4. Should a Christian ever actively disobey the state? Is there biblical support for civil disobedience? What does Lynn Buzzard suggest as guidelines for this difficult topic?

5. What are some inferences, according to the author, for a Christian living in a democracy?
6. What is the "political illusion"? What guidelines does Robert Dugan suggest for Christian involvement in politics?
7. Should the church as a local body ever support a political candidate? Should it form a political caucus? Summarize the author's points.

9

The Ethical Challenge of War and Capital Punishment

WAR AND CAPITAL punishment are perhaps the most excruciating ethical challenges for the Christian. As chapters 4 and 5 have shown, life is of infinite value to God and must always be respected and valued. Yet many Christians argue that it is proper and just to engage in war and kill other human beings created in God's image. Furthermore, Christians are involved in making and then deploying weapons of mass destruction. Is this justifiable in terms of God's Word? Finally, many Christians argue strongly for the right of the state to take the life of another human being who commits premeditated murder and other especially heinous crimes. How do we approach these difficult questions biblically?

A MATTER OF DEFINITION

The difference between *kill* and *murder* is critical in a discussion about war. Many Christians do not see a difference between these two terms, but the Bible does. The King James Version renders Exodus 20:13 as "Thou shalt not kill," while the New International Version renders the same verse, "You shall not murder." The Hebrew term in this case, *rasah*, does mean to kill, but it is never used in relation to animals and is always associated with murder. Furthermore, it is never used of killing an enemy in battle.[1] Therefore, not all life-taking is murder.

Two examples exist in the Old Testament. First is Genesis 9:6: "Whoever sheds man's blood, by man his blood shall be shed, for in the image of God He made man." God gave this principle to Noah before the Mosaic Law, and it was restated in Numbers 35 as part of the Mosaic Code. As Charles Ryrie states, "One can conclude that when the theocracy [of Israel] took the life of a murderer (i.e., one who violated the sixth commandment) the state (and particularly those who actually performed the execution) was not guilty of murder."[2] The second example is the conquest of Canaan. In Deuteronomy 20:10-18, God revealed His rules for war. It is clear from these regulations that Israel was not guilty of murder because they were the instruments of God's holy judgment.

Within the evangelical community there are three major positions on the problem of war. Each is defended biblically and held by committed Christians. The purpose of this part of the chapter is to review each position and offer the biblical defense of each. A short critique closes each section.

BIBLICAL PACIFISM

This position is based on God's call to be Christ's disciple. The Christian is to accept the person and teachings of Jesus and follow in His footsteps, regardless of the consequences. This includes Jesus' command to love your enemies. The goal of biblical pacifism is to lead people to a saving knowledge of Jesus Christ, bringing reconciliation with God and others and becoming ministers of the gospel of reconciliation to everyone. This goal, the pacifist argues, cannot be attained while at the same time participating in a program of ill will, retaliation, or war.

For the pacifist, the Old Testament does not justify war any more than it does polygamy or slavery. Christ came as the fulfillment of the Law, and He is God's final message. John Drescher, a defender of biblical pacifism, humorously states that the Christian cannot say, "Love your enemies [except in wartime]; Put up the sword in its place, for all that take the sword shall perish with the sword [except when the government tells me to fight]; If a man says, 'I love God,' and hates his brother, he is a liar [except when he fights in a war]; Bless those who persecute you, bless and curse not [except when my country is at war]."[3]

Killing is wrong, the pacifist categorically declares. That is the point of Exodus 20:13, buttressed with Jesus' words in Matthew 5:39: "Do not resist an evil person." The Christian is always to take the higher moral ground by protecting and securing human life. That is why war, to the pacifist, is simply mass murder, whether done within one's own society or in another. Instead, Christians are to love enemies, not kill them, which is the simple point of Matthew 5:44 and Romans 12:19-21. Myron Augsburger, a stern pacifist, declares that

Jesus "never sanctioned war, never approved violence." Instead, His "every word and action repudiated man's way of hate, murder, violence and self-defense. . . ."[4]

For this reason, argues the pacifist, nonviolence is a higher form of resistance; that is, violence is not the only viable option. John Stott reviews a case from World War II to illustrate: "In his interviews with German generals after World War II, Liddell-Hart found that 'violent forms of resistance had not been very effective or troublesome to them,' for they knew how to cope with these. But they had been baffled and disconcerted by the nonviolent resistance which they encountered in Denmark, Holland and Norway."[5] War breeds more war, and it means Christians will kill other Christians, a reprehensible option for Christ's disciples.

The major New Testament support for pacifism is the Sermon on the Mount. Jesus addressed people who were under oppressive foreign occupation. He did not advocate political revolution but only spiritual revolution. Jesus demanded active peacemaking—like going the extra mile—which could change the oppression and vengeful hatred into a new relationship of willful service and reconciliation. Furthermore, His life was characterized by love and nonviolence in His relationships with people and in His death. He, therefore, demonstrated the way of peace. This is powerfully illustrated in His statement: "My kingdom is not of this world. If My kingdom were of this world, then My servants would be fighting . . . but as it is, My kingdom is not of this realm" (John 18:36).

In Romans 13, Paul declares that authorities are established by God and that the believer is to be submissive to government commands as long as these do not violate God's laws. If obedience to God conflicts with human authority, Christians must be willing to bear the consequences as Christ and His disciples did. Full allegiance must be to God first. The New Testament relationship between Christians and the state is to "pray for and honor always, to overthrow never, and to obey when not in conflict with God's will."[6]

Scripture lays out clearly the pacifist lifestyle. To kill a non-Christian in war would be taking away any further opportunity for that person to be saved from sin. Christians are to sacrifice their lives for their brother, not kill him. For Christians to be fighting Christians is to make Caesar lord, not Jesus.[7] Believers are to love their enemies. If force is necessary, it must be imposed in such a manner that reconciliation will result. The gospel forbids force that results in death. God's children put their faith to work by giving help to the needy and bearing one another's burdens. This is the opposite of militarism. The Christian is a peacemaker. Menno Simons argued:

> The regenerated do not go to war, nor engage in strife. They are the children of peace who have beaten their swords into plowshares and their spears into pruning hooks and know of no war. Since we are to be conformed to the image of Christ, how can we then fight our enemies with the sword? Spears and swords of iron we leave to those who, alas, consider human blood and swine's blood of well-nigh equal value.[8]

CHRISTIAN ACTIVISM

This view represents the conviction that it is right to participate in war; it is the conviction, "my country, right or wrong." Governments are given authority to punish evil in both the Old Testament and the New Testament. Genesis 9:5-6 is the beginning of government with the authority to shed blood, presumably to deal with other nations who commit aggression and violence. Another key biblical passage is Romans 13:1-7, which for this position argues that government is established by God, and Christians must therefore submit. Verse 4 sees the ruler as a "minister" of God who "wields the sword" for justice. Since the obligation of the Christian is submission to the state, and since the state has the responsibility to use force, Christians should fight.[9] Personal feelings really play no role at all.

For the activist, government is the only guarantee of order and security. If there is no government, there will be anarchy. Thus, individuals who share the benefits of government must also share in its defense when that is necessary. It is just, according to this position, for the citizen to fulfill this obligation. Partial or total refusal to participate in defending the nation and obeying the government will further lead to anarchy and chaos. Citizens cannot, therefore, be given the freedom to choose to participate or not participate in war.

The major challenge for this view is when the state's commands contradict God's commands. When the apostles were charged by the Sanhedrin not to preach the gospel, they responded, "we must obey God rather than men" (Acts 5:29). Similarly, in the Old Testament, Shadrach, Meshach, and Abednego disobeyed an order to bow down to an idol

(Dan. 3), as did Daniel when he was ordered not to pray (Dan. 6). These several biblical examples demonstrate the weakness of the activist position. The Christian obeys government until it is a sin to do so.

THE JUST WAR TRADITION

Pacifism and activism are the two extremes on the war issue. Pacifism says it is not right to participate in war; activism says it is right and necessary. Through the history of the church, a mediating view has developed called the just war tradition. This tradition sees some wars as unjust and some as just. The challenge lies in discerning which wars are just.

Since the time of the fifth-century theologian Augustine, the majority of Christians have accepted the proposition that a set of criteria exists whereby a war and its methods are deemed just. What follows is a summary of the most widely accepted criteria for the just war tradition:

1. *A just cause*—A just cause for the use of force exists whenever it is necessary either to repel an unjust attack, to retake something wrongly taken, or to punish evil. An example of this criterion is Saddam Hussein's invasion of Kuwait in 1990. Ethically speaking, just war theorists argue, Saddam's action was a flagrant case of aggression, and therefore it was justifiable for the world community to repel his unjust aggression.

2. *Right authority*—This criterion focuses on established, legitimate, and properly constituted authority using force for a "just cause." In the United States this "right authority" consists in the powers granted to the President of the United States, by the War Powers Act or by a congressional declaration of war. In international affairs today, "right authority" might involve action by the UN Security Council authorizing the use of force. The point of this criterion focuses on legitimate authority, not private individuals who wage war.

3. *Right intention*—This criterion stresses the end goal for the use of force. The aim must be, for example, to turn back or undo aggression and then to deter such aggression in the future. The end for the use of force must be peace, not aggression or continued war. Again, the Gulf War of 1991 offers an example of this just war criterion. The world community had no aggressive aims against the territory or people of Iraq. "Right intention" in this conflict meant rolling back Saddam's aggression, establishing the peace of the Middle East, and assuring that safeguards would protect that peace in the future.

4. *Proportionate means*—As a criterion, this point centers on just

means in the use of force; it must be appropriate to the goal. For example, allowing aggression to stand, this view argues, is condoning an evil in itself and opening the door to yet further evil. Therefore, military force, whether land, air, or sea forces are involved, must be proportionate to the goal. Using nuclear weapons, for example, would be disproportionate in rolling back aggression of an underdeveloped nation with no air force or navy. Using chemical and biological weapons is another example of disproportionate means.

5. *Last resort*—This criterion involves the legitimate government using all diplomatic and foreign policy resources, including economic sanctions, to force the aggressive nation to pull back. If the aggressor responds with intransigence and continued belligerence, the legitimate government has no choice but use of military force. Again, the Iraq crisis of 1990-1991 offers a classic example of this criterion: The allies used economic sanctions, diplomatic activity, and personal diplomacy to change Saddam Hussein's aggressive actions against Kuwait. He refused. Therefore, just war advocates argue, the world community was just in rolling back his aggressive actions.

6. *Reasonable chance of success*—A war cannot be just unless there is some prospect of success. Otherwise lives will be needlessly taken in pursuit of a hopeless cause.

7. *Noncombatant immunity*—This is the most difficult criterion for the just war position. The military force must not directly use noncombatants in war or intentionally target them. Of course this means going to all ends not to intentionally and indiscriminately attack civilians or bomb civilian neighborhoods.

With the advent of weapons of mass destruction, whether nuclear or chemical or biological, one sees how difficult this criterion becomes for modern warfare. Noncombatant immunity does not exist. Because entire populations are decimated, neither does proportionate means. This is why many Christians argue that nuclear warfare does not meet this just war criterion and is therefore immoral and a sin.[10]

In summary, the just war position argues that war must be fought only for a just cause and not to pursue aggrandizement, glory, or vengeance. War must be declared by a legitimate authority and have a reasonable chance of success. The resulting good must outweigh the evil of warfare and of allowing the wrongdoing that provokes the war to continue. War must be a last resort after less violent approaches have failed. Civilian populations must not be deliberately attacked, every effort must be made to minimize casualties among them, and no unnec-essary force may be wielded against either troops or civilians.

Those who support this tradition give the following biblical pas-sages as support:

1. *Genesis 9:6*—Here we find part of the Noahic covenant where God delineates the responsibility of humans to be instruments of His justice. With the killing of humans comes the responsibility of holding the murderer accountable. This, by inference, is what nations must do as well—hold aggressors and perpetrators of international violence accountable, even if it means using military force.

2. *Matthew 22:21; 1 Timothy 2:1-2; Titus 3:1; 1 Peter 2:13*—In these passages, Christians are called upon to practice civil obedience to prop-erly constituted authority. As stated earlier in this chapter, this is not blind obedience, for when human law conflicts with God's law, the Christian obeys God.

3. *Romans 13:4*—In this classic passage, God delegates to the state the responsibility to use the sword as an instrument of justice and to punish evil. By extension, this tradition holds that nations must use mil-itary force to promote justice and punish evil.

4. *John 18:11; Luke 22:36*—In these passages Jesus deals with the use of the sword as an instrument of self-defense. In the first He rebukes Peter for his misuse of the sword; He does not condemn the use of the sword in self-defense. In the Luke passage, Jesus seems to be allowing for a legitimate use of the sword for self-defense when, in light of His rejection, He instructs His disciples: "let him who has no sword sell his robe and buy one." Again, by inference, nations acting in self-defense are justified in using military force.

There is enormous tension in thinking about the just war tradition. Yet because we live in a sin-cursed world, it is probably the wisest choice among the three major options. But it should never soothe or bring com-fort! Thinking about this tradition and then its implementation should always vex and trouble. If a nation fights what it has determined to be a just war, it must never do so with arrogance and bombastic pride; instead, it must fight with tears and with agonizing tension. War should never be easy. It remains one of the most perplexing ethical issues for the Christian.

CAPITAL PUNISHMENT

As with the issue of war, the question of capital punishment is filled with intellectual and theological tension. This section does not deal with how capital punishment is practiced in the United States or any other country. Instead, the focus is whether one can make a biblical defense of capital punishment as a responsibility of the state. If humans bear God's image (Gen. 1:26-27), then taking the life of an image-bearer in a premeditated act of murder ethically demands just punishment. Murdering a human being is an attack on the Creator God. It is a rejection of His sovereignty over human life (Deut. 32:39). But is it just to make the punishment capital? This section will argue yes.

Several key biblical passages make the case for capital punishment as a just obligation of the state:

1. *Genesis 9:6*—As Noah exits the ark, God establishes a new relationship with the human race and a new code on which to base human relationships. Because of the Flood's destruction of all life, future generations might conclude that life is cheap to God and assume that humans can destroy life also. However, the new code affirmed the sacredness of human life and held that murder is punishable by death. The text, therefore, institutes the principle of *talionic* justice, or law of like punishment. Talionic justice is not harsh, for it establishes the premise that the punishment should fit the crime. This principle is summarized elsewhere in God's Word as "eye for eye, tooth for tooth" (Exod. 21:23-25). The point of this covenant with Noah is that God removed justice from the hands of the family of the deceased and gave it to human government, eliminating the personal revenge factor and emotional anger.

2. *The Mosaic Law*—God's moral law revealed to Moses was not the first time God delegated the authority of capital punishment. This authority is central to Genesis 9:6 and is clearly implied in Genesis 4 in God's dialogue with Cain (vv. 10, 14). What God did with the Mosaic Law was to broaden the responsibility to include many other offenses: murder (Exod. 21:12; Num. 35:16-31), working on the Sabbath (Exod. 35:2), cursing father and mother (Lev. 20:9), adultery (Lev. 20:10), incest (Lev. 20:11-12), sodomy (Lev. 20:13, 15-16), false prophesying (Deut. 13:1-10; 18:20), idolatry (Exod. 20:4), rape (Deut. 22:25), keeping an ox that has killed a human being (Exod. 21:29), kidnapping (Exod. 21:16), and intrusion of an alien into a sacred place (Num. 1:51; 3:10, 38). The form of execution was normally stoning or burning.[11]

3. *Romans 13:1-7*—Verse 4 is the key verse in this critical section

on the authority of the state in our lives. It gives the state the authority to wield the "sword" in its role as the punisher of evil: "it [the civil ruler] does not bear the sword for nothing; for it is a minister of God, an avenger who brings wrath on the one who practices evil." The word used for sword here is *machaira*, which refers not only to a sword used in battle, but also to a sword used in executions, as when Herod killed James, the brother of John, in Acts 12:1-2.[12] Paul's use of this word gives strong support to the idea that the state receives from God the authority to execute. It gives no help in deciding which crimes are capital offenses.

In summary, the principle of talionic justice, implied in Genesis 4:10, 14, was clearly instituted in Genesis 9:6 and reaffirmed quite broadly in the Mosaic Law. It is likewise power delegated to the state according to Romans 13:4. The New Testament did not negate the Old Testament standard of capital punishment. The continuity of the Testaments is affirmed.

IS CAPITAL PUNISHMENT A DETERRENT?

Both the criminal justice system and theologians are divided as to whether capital punishment deters criminal behavior. When comparing crime rates of states that use capital punishment to those that do not, it is impossible to argue that capital punishment is a deterrent. Statistics can be stated to posit whatever you want them to say. But from the perspective of Scripture, this is beside the point.

The view of capital punishment defended in this chapter gives focus to the fundamental biblical reason for capital punishment. Specifically, killing another human (an image-bearer of God) demands taking the murderer's life based on the principle of talionic justice. Whether this form of justice deters further murders is almost irrelevant to the issue. Justice demands payment. The universal and binding principle that God instituted in Genesis 9:6 is as applicable today as it was in Noah's day.

In conclusion, whether one is thinking about war or about capital punishment, enormous tension exists. Neither issue is simple. This chapter has suggested the just war tradition as a possible way of reducing some of the tension on the issue of war. It has also defended the matter of capital punishment as an issue of justice. Both war and capital punishment are carried out with remorse and tears, looking to God for wisdom and discernment.

FOR FURTHER DISCUSSION

1. Explain the use of the term *kill* in Exodus 20:13.
2. Summarize in one sentence the three views of war:
   • pacifism
   • activism
   • just war
3. Summarize in detail the biblical passages used to defend pacifism and activism.
4. List and explain the criteria used to defend the just war tradition.
5. Summarize in detail the biblical defense of the just war tradition.
6. Explain how each of the following was used in the defense of the biblical principle of capital punishment:
   • Genesis 4:10, 14
   • Genesis 9:6
   • Talionic justice
   • Romans 13:4
7. In the author's opinion how important is the issue of deterrence to the question of capital punishment?

10

The Ethics of Work and Race

SOME PEOPLE HATE to do it. Some love to do it. Some go to great lengths to avoid doing it. Some do it too much. While there are many different attitudes toward work, one thing remains constant: Work must be done. Since the Garden of Eden everyone has worked or depended on someone else's work for their survival. Furthermore, work sets a person's lifestyle—where to live, when to sleep and eat, time with family, and even dress. If a person is not content with work, the rest of life is in turmoil. What should be the Christian's attitude toward work? Is it a blessing or a curse? Is work a means to justify the ends of leisure and entertainment? This chapter focuses on developing a Christian work ethic and discussing the proper perspective on work relationships.

A BIBLICAL VIEW OF WORK

Work is ordained by God. It was His creative invention from the beginning. While we do not usually think of God as working, and while we do not know all the details, the Bible declares that God worked (Gen. 1—2). By working, we resemble God. Like God, humans have the ability to work, make plans, implement them, and be creative. In addition, Genesis 1:28 and 2:15 proclaim that God gave humans the task of ruling over and taking care of His creation. Theologian Carl Henry writes:

> Through his work, man shares the creation purpose of God in subduing nature, whether he is a miner with dirty hands, a mechanic with a greasy face, or a stenographer with stencil smudged fingers. Work is permeated by purpose; it is intended to serve God, benefit mankind, make nature subservient to the moral program for cre-

ation. Man must therefore apply his whole being—heart and mind, as well as hand—to the daily job. As God's fellow worker he is to reflect God's creative ability on Monday in the factory no less than on Sunday when commemorating the day of rest and worship.[1]

Apparently Adam and Eve's pre-Fall work had both a physical and spiritual dimension. With respect to the Garden of Eden, God told them "to cultivate it and keep it" (Gen. 2:15). The Hebrew word translated "keep" is used in 3:24, referring to the angel who was "to guard the way to the tree of life." Adam and Eve had that same responsibility, an immense spiritual stewardship, before their rebellion against God. Therefore, work has both a physical and a spiritual dimension.

Work is not only toilsome, due to sin, but it is for a lifetime. Genesis 3:19 says, "By the sweat of your face you shall eat bread, till *you return to the ground*" (emphasis added). Apparently God intends that humans are to work as long as they live. Meaningful activity plays a critical role in what we are as human beings. Retirement does not end work; rather it must include work—for a person's overall well-being. This proposition speaks volumes about the manner in which Western civilization views the retirement years. The magical age of sixty-five should not end meaningful, purposeful work.

When interpreting Genesis 3:17-19, some argue that work is a curse resulting from the Fall. While God's curse in these verses has an enormous effect on work, work itself is not a punishment. God's point is that pain and toil are involved when humans seek productive results. In addition, counteracting forces tend to restrict those results. Until death, humans are always faced with painful, laborious toil. God did not create work as drudgery; that is the result of sin. Therefore, we speak today of "getting back to the grind" or to the "salt mine." Work today is tedious, difficult, and often frustrating.

Despite the "painful toil," work has three basic purposes: to meet human needs, to provide for a quality of life, and to serve (and worship) God. First, work provides money (or resources) to supply the necessities of life. Jesus said that it is proper to pray for our "daily bread" (Matt. 6:11), and a way that prayer is answered is through work. Second, work enhances the quality of life. Work enhances the satisfaction of life and is the strongest predictor of life span, even above general happiness and other physical factors.[2]

Furthermore, psychological and mental health are related to work.

A person receives a sense of personal dignity and worth from work. Most Americans, when introducing themselves, share their name and occupation. People who are without work often suffer from depression, poor self-image, and mental illnesses.[3] God gave work as a gift of fulfillment in life. The worker is to enjoy it for more than simply its economic benefits. Ecclesiastes 2:24-25 (NIV) argues that a human being "can do nothing better than . . . find satisfaction in his work. This too, I see, is from the hand of God, for without him, who can eat or find enjoyment?"

The final purpose of work is to serve God. Colossians 3:22—4:1 is the major biblical passage on the proper ethical attitude for work. Here Paul writes to slaves and masters. However, remember that the vast majority of workers in the Roman Empire were slaves, working usually for life with limited rights. In many ways, the slave's relationship to his master is similar to the employee/employer relationship of today.

In this passage, the apostle Paul details three principles on the ethic of work. First is the principle of obedience, consistency, and sincerity (Col. 3:22). The Christian is to approach work as a matter of obedience to God; it is a stewardship from Him that demands a commitment of obedience and a consistency even when the boss is not looking. Christian workers likewise approach the job sincerely, in a conscientious manner. The second principle is the lordship of Jesus Christ; Christian workers serve "the Lord Christ" (Col. 3:23-24). One could easily argue that our real boss is Jesus Christ. We work for Him, and we are to see our work as service to Him, not simply to our employer. Finally, verse 24 states that the reason Christians maintain such a high work ethic is because we know God will reward us. In other words, there is eternal significance to work. Part of God's reward system involves reward for our work. What would happen to the quality of products and to productivity if all workers viewed work according to the standards of Colossians 3?

From this chapter so far, it would seem that people should be excited about the idea of going to work. Yet the opposite is true. Strikes, low productivity, union demands, absenteeism, and high turnover rates are symptoms of dissatisfied workers. Due to sin, the meaning of work has become distorted and twisted. The goal of work today is to enjoy the end product and work only because it is a means to that end— leisure. Even Christians fall into this mind-set. Leisure is not *the end*. Work, as this chapter has shown, is the end in itself. It is a stewardship from God, and how we approach it has eternal implications.

IMPLICATIONS OF A CHRISTIAN WORK ETHIC

From the argument presented in this chapter, it is possible to deduce several implications for a Christian work ethic:

1. Everyone should work. Since God ordained work, humans will only find fulfillment in working. It is the key to finding purpose in life.

2. Excellence is the worker's standard. Ephesians 6:6-7 exhorts the Christian to "render service, as to the Lord, and not to men," not to be men-pleasers but God-pleasers. God's standard of excellence needs to be the human standard.

3. Respect and obedience are to characterize workers. Both Colossians and Ephesians challenge the slave (employee) to show respect to the master (employer). The master (employer) is likewise to show respect and treat kindly the slave (employee). Love, mutual respect, and justice must characterize the employer/employee relationship.

4. All professions and all kinds of work, assuming they are legal and biblically ethical, are honorable before the Lord. There simply is no dichotomy between sacred and secular work. All work brings glory to God and fulfillment to the human if it is done to God's glory (1 Cor. 10:31).

5. Work provides an opportunity for a witness. As the disciple of Christ follows a Christian work ethic, he or she manifests a powerful message, both verbal and nonverbal, of a supernatural approach to work. The world today needs this powerful witness.

6. Work is actually a form of worship. Such an attitude cultivates honesty, integrity, and excellence.

In conclusion, the gospel of Jesus Christ brings total transformation to the human being. It brings personal responsibility, dignity, and purpose—core values for a productive, God-centered work ethic. The Christian's daily job is a daily offering to God. This is a transformational, supernatural, eternally significant perspective on the mundane chore called work.

THE ETHICS OF RACE

America has a history littered with ugly manifestations of the sin of racism. Principally, the United States institutionalized chattel slavery, which was fundamentally racist in its orientation; it centered on the enslavement of Africans. It took the bitter and costly Civil War (1861-1865) to destroy this monstrous evil. Many years have passed since the Civil Rights Acts of 1964 and 1965, which freed African-Americans from legalized segregation, denial of voting rights, and blanket discrimination in the labor market. Racial identification of any kind no longer presents a hindrance to voting privileges. The African-American representation in the House of Representatives is now approaching its proportion to the total population. Although minorities (particularly African-American) are far from economic parity with Caucasians, high positions in government, the military, business, and education are attainable for them.

Nevertheless, almost everyone agrees that something remains wrong, and the dream of Martin Luther King, Jr., for an integrated society where people would be judged by character rather than color has not been fully realized. Racism, in all its ugliness, remains a part of American society. What does God's Word say about race? How should we view people of a different color? What is the biblical solution to the ongoing remnants of racism toward all minorities in America?

There are several biblical passages critical to forming Christ-mindedness on the subject of race:

1 Corinthians 1:18—The apostle Paul establishes that from God's viewpoint there are only two groups of human beings: those who are with Christ and those who are without Christ—in other words, those who have trusted Jesus Christ as Savior and those who have not. The Bible does not allow for racial differences as a basis for discrimination or ranking of humans. Jesus' death on Calvary's cross was for *all* of humanity—red, black, brown, yellow, and white.

Genesis 9:20-27—Historically, this passage has been used to justify the enslavement of the black race that occurred in the United States after 1619. Since some of Ham's descendants populated Africa, Noah's curse (some conclude) must therefore apply to all those who are from Africa. Many in the southern part of the United States prior to the Civil War used this argument to justify racial slavery. Unfortunately this perception about Noah's curse remains today.

The behavior of Noah after the Flood provided the occasion for Ham's sin. There is a remarkable contrast between Noah's conduct before the Flood and after. Noah, who walked in righteousness with God, planted a vineyard, became drunk, and lay naked in his tent. Unfortunately, since the Fall, drunkenness or nakedness can lead to personal slavery or decadence!

Noah's actions induce Ham's sin. Verse 22 states that Ham "saw the nakedness of his father, and told his two brothers." Despite many interpretations, there is no clear evidence that Ham did anything other than see his father's nakedness. As Allen Ross makes clear, "Nakedness in the Old Testament was from the beginning a thing of shame for fallen humankind. For Adam and Eve as sinners, the state of nakedness was both undignified and vulnerable. . . .To be exposed meant to be unprotected; to see someone uncovered was to bring dishonor and to gain advantage for potential exploitation."[4] By stressing that Ham entered and saw Noah's nakedness, Genesis depicts Ham's looking as a moral flaw, a first step in the abandonment of a moral code. In the words of Ross, "Ham desecrated a natural and sacred barrier. His going to tell his brothers about it without covering the old man aggravated the act."[5]

But Noah's curse in verses 25-27 was on Ham's youngest son, Canaan, that Canaan would be a "servant of servants" (i.e., slavery). Noah's curse anticipated in Canaan the evil traits that marked his father Ham and so judged him. The text prepares the reader by twice mentioning that Ham was Canaan's father, signifying more than lineage. To the Hebrew mind, the Canaanites were the most natural embodiment of Ham. "Everything the Canaanites did in their pagan existence was symbolized by the attitude of Ham. From the moment the patriarchs entered the land, these tribes were their corrupting influence."[6] The constant references to "nakedness" and "uncovering" in Leviticus 18 designate a people enslaved sexually, reminding Israel of the sin of Ham. These descendants of Ham were not cursed because of what Ham did; they were cursed because they acted as their ancestor did.[7]

In conclusion, it is simply impossible to see any justification for slavery or any type of inferiority from the curse on Canaan. It is a gross distortion of God's Word to do so. Furthermore, as Charles Ryrie affirms, "it is [also] irrelevant today since it would be difficult, if not impossible, to identify a Canaanite."[8]

Acts 10:34-35—The point of this extraordinary passage is that the salvation God offers is to all humans everywhere, regardless of racial background or characteristics. Peter learns that ". . . God does not show favoritism but accepts men from every nation who fear him and do what is right" (NIV). Racial hatred or discrimination is impossible when one sees people the way God does.

James 2:1-9—The story is told of Mahatma Gandhi's search for truth and harmony for his people of India. Raised a Hindu, Gandhi did not believe that Hinduism offered the solution to the horrendous discrimination and rigid caste system of India. As he studied law in South Africa, he believed that Christianity might have the answer. Hoping to find in Christianity what Hinduism lacked, he attended a church in South Africa. Because the South African church embraced the system of racial segregation called apartheid, the usher offered him a seat on the floor. Gandhi decided that he might as well remain a Hindu, for Christianity has its own caste system as well. What a tragedy!

James 2 will have none of this. James decries the typical situation of the early church where the wealthy were given a place of privilege and honor in worship, while the poor were only permitted to sit on the floor. Such discriminatory practices violate God's royal law: "Love your neighbor as yourself." To show favoritism is sin; it desecrates God's standard of love.

The church of Jesus Christ should therefore model the supernatural impartiality that refuses to discriminate. The church should model reconciliation of all races and ethnic groups. It should cut the radical path for all of society, for it alone sees people the way God sees them: Whatever race or ethnic background, all need Jesus Christ, and all bear His image. The church has the radical solution to society's struggle with racial and ethnic differences. It is a supernatural solution—disciples of Jesus Christ who have experienced His salvation and who love one another with the supernatural love of their Savior. All the world needs to see this radical solution lived out.

FOR FURTHER DISCUSSION

1. Show from Scripture that work predated the Fall of Adam and Eve into sin.
2. In what sense does work have a spiritual dimension? Explain.
3. What does the author argue are the three purposes for work?
4. From Colossians 3:21—4:1, summarize the apostle Paul's three principles for work.
5. List and describe the author's six implications of a Christian work ethic.
6. Using the following Scripture passages, show that racism is a sin:
   • 1 Corinthians 1:18
   • Acts 10:34-35
   • James 2:1-9
7. How would you respond to someone who says the "curse of Ham" mentioned in Genesis 9 proves that black enslavement was part of God's plan? Be sure to focus on a proper understanding of Genesis 9:20-27.

11

The Christian, the Arts, and Entertainment

TODAY THE ARTS—both performing and visual—are often ignored by the church of Jesus Christ. Rarely do evangelical Christians attend art museums, classical music concerts, or ballet. Such enterprises are often considered secular and unworthy of Christian involvement. The result is that the arts are almost exclusively in the domain of the world; very few Christians are in leadership positions in the arts; nor do they participate in the visual or performing arts. This is a tragedy, for God is a God of beauty, and He desires that His creatures reflect His commitment to beauty as well. That is certainly part of being in the image of God.

Franky Schaeffer, in a highly provocative book, *Addicted to Mediocrity*, argues that Christians have sacrificed the artistic prominence they enjoyed for centuries and have settled for mediocrity. Today "Christian" doodads, trinkets, clothing, and bumper stickers are the major contribution Christians make to creative expression. This is a sad state of affairs. Christians need to be involved in the arts. To neglect this area is to surrender a pivotal opportunity for influence (e.g., the medieval cathedrals).

CREATIVITY—A CHRISTIAN CONCEPT

When the Christian thinks of creativity, it is usually in the context of the arts. Those with artistic ability are said to be "creative types," while the untalented look on with envy. But this attitude is totally unbiblical. Creativity is basic to life. God is a God of beauty, creativity, and variety; one need only look at His physical creation for proof. We bear His image (Gen. 1:26), and creativity is a part of being in the image of God.

Definition of Creativity

Peter Angeles defines *creation* as "bringing something new into existence out of something previously existing."[1] *Creation*, the noun, refers to the act of creation or the product of the act. *Creative*, the adjective, refers to the quality one possesses to create. The verb form is transitive, meaning "to produce, to give rise to something." Several conclusions flow from this definition:

1. Creativity is not quantitative but qualitative.

2. Creativity is a process that involves movement, progression, and change. There is no single creative act, only creative action. Painting a picture involves many acts; taken as a whole, painting is a process.

3. Because creativity is a quality and a process, it cannot be measured. The only way to "see" creativity is through its effects (e.g., paintings, compositions, sculptures, etc.).

4. Because *create* is a transitive verb, it always has an object. Thus, the creative process always has a product. The composer produces a composition, the painter a painting, and the sculptor a sculpture. The product of Genesis 1:1 is the universe.

5. Finally, creativity is an actualizing of potential. Things that exist have the potential to be rearranged, put together, or simply become different.

Biblical Principles of Creativity

Rooted in the proposition that God is the Creator and we are His creatures, the following principles provide the basis for thinking and acting biblically when it comes to creativity. Such a foundation, then, enables the Christian to gain an appreciation for and an involvement in the arts.

1. Human creativity derives its value from God's creativity. In Genesis 1:26-30, after God had finished His creative work, He detailed His creation mandate for humanity. Humans are to subdue and have dominion over His creation.

2. Human creativity manifests God's image. Bearing God's image means that we carry His creativity into our human capacity for sensory, intellectual, and emotional delight.

3. Creativity is to be developed in all persons, not just a creative elite. Since all bear His image, all have some dimension of creativity.

4. Creativity extends to all cultural activities, including art, science, work, play, thought, and action. One of the clear teachings of God's

Word is the lordship of Jesus Christ. If He is Lord of all, then that lordship extends to all dimensions of life.

5. Human creativity exists for the glory of God. First Corinthians 10:31 makes clear that we are to do all to the glory of God. Each time we exercise our creative potential, we are giving glory to the one who created and gifted us. All praise to Him![2]

Characteristics of the Creative Christian

What follows is a list of characteristics that foster creativity. It is not exhaustive, merely suggestive. The list is rooted in the proposition that God is creative, and so are His creatures.

1. The creative person is well rounded. This means that creativity is exercised in all areas of life—social, intellectual, spiritual, and psychological. The growing Christian is a balanced person developing all of life's aspects.

2. The creative person is curious. Curiosity is eager to learn and grow. When we realize that all aspects of creation are God's, then our goal is to understand *all* of God's creation. Our propensity to inquire and to learn produces creativity.

3. The creative person is courageous. It takes courage to learn a new subject, to explore a new area of knowledge, or to do a new activity (e.g., painting, music, ballet). To be bold and courageous goes hand in hand with creativity.

4. The creative person is humble. The realization of absolute dependence on God is the beginning of creativity. All gifts or talents come from God, and we exercise them for His glory. Humility and a proper understanding of self are the keys to the proper exercise of God's gifts.

CHRISTIANITY AND THE ARTS

Many evangelicals have a vague discomfort about the arts. They are uncertain whether or not art has any meaningful value. They are confused about where it fits into God's priorities.

This confusion and misunderstanding further results in one of two attitudes about art: either antagonism or neglect. Gordon Jackson observes, "Whether by the activism of hostility and antagonism . . . or by the passivity of inaction and neglect, the outcome is the same: there is within evangelical circles minimal patronage of the arts, and even less interest in integrating that segment of culture with the Christian faith."

Cultural illiteracy, Jackson argues, is one result; little production of quality art by evangelical Christians is another. For example, he noted that out of an estimated thirty-three million church-going evangelicals in the United States, "not even one outstanding novelist has emerged."[3]

The Value of Art

Novelist and playwright Dorothy Sayers notes that the very first thing we learn about God is that He *creates*.[4] Indeed, as the Creator of the universe, God is the ultimate example of creative expression: "If from this world around us we can learn anything about God's character, surely it is that we have a creative God, a God of diversity, a God whose interest in beauty and detail must be unquestioned when one looks at the world which he has made around us, and people themselves as the result of his craftsmanship."[5]

God creates for usefulness, enjoyment, and even as a means of revealing His character. Some aspects of His creation are beautiful exhibitions of His creativity and yet are never seen by humans. Philip Yancey asks the question: "Why is it that the most beautiful animals on earth are hidden away from all humans except those wearing scuba equipment? Who are they beautiful for?"[6] Evidently, their beauty is for God alone. Schaeffer remarks, "we live in a world full of 'useless' beauty."[7] Therefore, art and beauty have intrinsic value.

As this chapter has already noted, because we are God's image-bearers, we are taken "deep into the nature of our human creative ability. For one of the marks of the image of God that we bear is that we, too, in our creaturely way, are makers. And in no human activity is this aspect of God's image more evident than in our making art."[8] Just as God's artwork needs no utilitarian justification, neither does ours; it has inherent value because it is given by God as part of His image. It is inherently good in His eyes.

A basic function of art is that it both expresses and shapes people's values and their worldview.[9] This is obvious because art usually deals with major issues: life and death, love and hate, etc. The worldview expressed in a culture's art reflects the worldview of that culture's people. Witness the impact of modern music and entertainment. That is why withdrawal from the arts is so potentially devastating for Christianity.

Schaeffer contends, "Any group that willingly or unconsciously sidesteps creativity and human expression gives up their effective role in the society in which they live. In Christian terms, their ability to be the salt of that society is greatly diminished."[10]

A related but slightly different value for artistic expression is that it offers insight into reality. Art communicates the familiar in a fresh, enlightening way. Art enables one to experience newfound insights into ourselves, others, and the world around him or her. For example, reading a well-written story about someone grieving over the death of one's father enables one to know what it is like to lose a father. A good painting of poverty enriches understanding of what it means to be poor.

Art likewise has emotional power. It is able to communicate one perspective of truth as nothing else can. For example, one of the best expressions of God's glory is Handel's *Messiah*. This work communicates that subjective element of truth like few other musical compositions.

The Value of Specific Art

Artists create works of art, and the diversity of literature, music, dance, cinema, and graphic arts is the result. Within these widely different fields each piece of art is unique and demands its own critique. If art in general is inherently valuable, is every work of art inherently valuable? Are all works of art equally valuable, or should their value be determined relative to certain standards?

Although human creative ability is part of bearing God's image, this image was marred through the Fall. Gaebelein reminds us, "No biblical thinker, whether in aesthetics or in any other field, can afford to slight the fact that, because of the fall, man has an innate bent toward sin, and that bent is reflected in what he does."[11]

Can such art really have inherent value, really be of inherent good in God's sight? If art has a great potential for good, it also has a great potential for evil. As products of fallen humanity, art is tainted by the human sin nature. As products of finite beings, art is an imperfect expression of the creative nature of God. What then should we do? What criteria should Christians use in evaluating art?

Allow me to suggest three basic criteria for evaluating art and beauty. First, is the artist skilled (achieving mastery in the medium)? Second, what is the content of the artwork (conveying truth, morals, or specific worldview)? Finally, how creative is the artwork (providing a fresh perspective)?

In each of the three criteria, God has an ideal for artistic beauty. In skill, He is pleased with excellence; in content, He is pleased with truth;

in creativity, He is pleased with quality and depth. Each of these criteria is a reflection of His character—excellence, truth, and creativity. Without trying to oversimplify this complex issue, it seems that the closer a piece of art is to these ideals, the more pleasing it is to God. But beauty remains nebulous, argues Gaebelein:

> . . . to justify beauty exclusively with harmony and orderliness does scant justice to the power and truth the arts are capable of. . . . Dissonance in music, stark realism in literature, and the "ugly" in visual art all have an indispensable relation to beauty. The concept of beauty in art must be large enough to include the aesthetic astringencies. For beauty wears different faces.[12]

To be a Christian is not to be taken out of the world and made a purely spiritual being. Rather, it is to be transformed into the image God had for humans at creation. Sanctification is the making of real humans. (See 1 Thess. 5:23, where the whole "spirit, soul, and body" are spoken of in relation to sanctification.) Rookmaaker argues that ". . . God is the God of life and . . . the Bible teaches people how to live, how to deal with our world, God's creation."[13] This certainly gives focus to the need for a biblical view of art. Such a focus is reflected in Calvin Seerveld's call for the church to recognize the value and necessity of art:

> This is my argument to you Christians: Given the contemporary situation of clenched despair and practical madness . . . how can you live openly in this world, God's cosmic theater of wonder, while the (common) graciously preserved unbelievers revel in music and drama, paintings, poetry and dance, with a riot of color, a deafening sound raised in praise to themselves and their false gods, how can you live openly and be silent? . . . That men of darkened understanding can make merry under God's nose and curse him with desperately, damnable forceful art should hurt you . . . only different art, not censorship, will take this antithesis earnestly and meet it.[14]

CHRISTIANITY AND ENTERTAINMENT

One of the greatest inhibitors of creative potential is television. According to Richard Zoglin, "except for school and family, no institution plays a bigger role in shaping the American child" than television.[15] The average American child will watch 5,000 hours of television before first grade and will have watched a total of 19,000 hours by the time of high school graduation. The lifetime total for television viewing is nine years by the age of sixty-five.[16] The average home today has the television on six hours and seventeen minutes a day!

The effect on the brain of watching television is staggering. Clement Walchshauser observes that "watching television produces highly altered brain wave states when people watch for a mere twenty minutes." It puts the brain into a totally passive condition unaware of its surroundings and lessening the attention span.[17] Obsessive television watching has further negative effects:

• *It demands our time.* It is nearly addictive as it draws the viewer in, resulting in less time spent serving God, family, or others.

• *It determines behavior.* A national report entitled *Television and Behavior* was issued by the National Institute of Health in 1982. The report, a summary of more than 2,500 studies conducted since 1972, demonstrated "overwhelming evidence of a causal link between children's watching television violence and their performance of violent acts."[18]

• *It distorts the perception of reality.* Children especially confuse real life with television life and values. A recent study discovered that 90 percent of boys surveyed would rather watch their favorite television program than spend time with their fathers. Quentin Schultze reports that ". . . the lure of the television is strong for young boys, who especially like the aggressive characters and automobile violence of the action shows."[19]

• *It dulls moral sensitivity.* A steady diet of soap operas, situation comedies, or movies desensitizes, enabling acceptance of what earlier would have been rejected (e.g., adultery, premarital sex, homosexuality, murder, violent rage). Obsessive viewing of such activities produces an acceptance and toleration of acts repugnant to God.

• *It destroys meaningful family life.* Time in front of the television set diminishes time for games, reading, music, etc. Watching television can be lethal to cultivating creativity.

Obsessive viewing of television, then, not only affects creative potential, but it may also produce significant negative behavior. Guidelines rooted in Scripture help us develop wise principles:

1. *The principle of stewardship of time* (Eph. 5:15-16)—Time is like any other commodity. We are accountable to God for what we do with it. This includes entertainment choices and the amount of time those choices require.

2. *The principle of control* (1 Cor. 6:12; Gal 5:23)—Self-control is a fruit of the Spirit. There is no greater test of this virtue than personal discipline in television and/or movie viewing.

3. *The principle of moral purity* (Phil. 4:8)— We must make the choice as to "whatever is true, . . . honorable, . . . right, . . . pure, . . . lovely, . . . of good repute, if there is any excellence and if anything worthy of praise, let your mind dwell on these things." These virtues form the grid to making wise entertainment choices.

4. *The principle of edification* (1 Cor. 10:23)—The believer in Jesus Christ has great freedom, but with that freedom comes immense responsibility. Although we may have the freedom to participate in many forms of entertainment, most of those forms may not build us up in the Christian faith. In fact, a regular diet of poor entertainment may actually tear down our faith.

5. *The principle of God's glory* (1 Cor. 10:31)—There are no exceptions on the overarching theme of this book that we do all for God's glory, including entertainment choices.

What then should Christians do? Entertainment choices are never easy. Yet in light of these principles several practical suggestions follow for wise decision-making:

• *Participate actively in entertainment choices.* Be a critical thinker. Always ask yourself, "How is this affecting me?" when it comes to entertainment. Passivity is unacceptable.

• *Be selective in choosing family entertainment.* The television or the movie theater are not the only choices. Consider visiting an art museum, a concert, or historical location. Also, consider reading a book out loud together as a family.

• *Read program descriptions for television and movies carefully and critically.* Prepare your children for what they will see and then discuss the entertainment content, themes, and worldview presented in the program or movie.

• *Log how much money is spent by the family on entertainment.* Periodically evaluate with the children whether too much is being spent.

• *Do not stare passively at commercials.* Discuss the product or persuasive content of the advertisement with one another.

• *Practice turning off the television.* Explain to your children that when a program offends or behavior is addictive, it is wise to exercise such self-control.

Psalm 101:2-3 seems most appropriate:

> *I will give heed to the blameless way . . .*
> *I will walk within my house in the integrity of my heart.*
> *I will set no worthless thing before my eyes;*
> *I hate the work of those who fall away;*
> *It shall not fasten its grip on me.*

FOR FURTHER DISCUSSION

1. How does the author define creativity? Do you agree? Offer your own definition.
2. List and elaborate upon the biblical principles of creativity. Cite some examples of each.
3. Comment on the author's contention that television is an enemy of creativity. Is he calling for the banning of television from Christian homes? Do you agree with his analysis?
4. List and summarize the biblical principles for making wise entertainment choices. How could you apply these in your own home?
5. List the practical guidelines for making wise entertainment decisions. Do you agree? Can you add any of your own?
6. The author argues that Christians are often confused about the role of art in their lives, which causes them to either treat art with antagonism or neglect. Explain what he means.
7. What does the author mean when he argues that art has intrinsic value and worth, not only utilitarian value?
8. Summarize the meaning of these purposes that art serves:
   - Art reflects a people's worldview.
   - Art reflects reality.
   - Art has emotional power.
9. List and explain the three criteria for art that pleases God.
10. What is your response to Seerveld's quote issuing a challenge to Christians?

The Christian and the Environment

IN TODAY'S WORLD many Christians are confused about environmental issues. Disciplined but unchastened Catholic theologian Matthew Fox says we should turn from a theology centered on sin and redemption to develop a creation spirituality, with nature as our primary revelation and sin as a distant memory. In 1967 historian Lynn White, Jr., argued that it is precisely the Christian view of persons and nature that created the whole ecological mess. Meanwhile, many evangelicals come close to celebrating the demise of planet Earth, enthusiastically citing the decay as proof of Christ's return.[1]

Complicating things further is the emergence of the doctrine of Gaia, most famously represented in Rosemary Ruether's book.[2] Ruether, a Catholic feminist theologian, argues that male domination of women and male domination of nature are interconnected. She defines *sin* as wrong relationships among people and between humans and the rest of nature. These distorted relationships foster not just economic and political injustice, racism, and sexism, but also threaten the destruction of the entire created order. The Gaia hypothesis holds that our planet is a living creature. The theory, in fact, imputes a kind of divine power to earth. Respect for the planet is the key to restoring the right relationships destroyed by male dominion.

What are we to think about all of this? Is Christianity to blame for the environmental crisis? As Christians, how are we to treat the physical world? What is the value of nonhuman life? How much responsibility do we as Christians have for nature? How does God look at nonhuman creation?

When my daughter, at about age six, was found outside systematically killing ants on the sidewalk, I asked her what she was doing. She responded, "Daddy, Mommy does not like ants; so I am killing them."

Sensing this was a teachable moment, I asked her, "Joanna, do you think God is pleased with killing ants like this? Are they in Mommy's cupboards? Are they hurting us here on the walk?" She did not know how to respond at first. Our subsequent talk focused on treating God's creatures with respect because God holds us accountable for managing His creation well. I doubt she understood all we discussed, but it began a process of teaching stewardship of God's creation.

In 1970 Francis Schaeffer published *Pollution and the Death of Man: The Christian View of Ecology*.[3] Much of the material in this chapter echoes his argument. Schaeffer's pioneering work continues to influence my thinking on the environment and my responsibility to God in this area.

INADEQUATE VIEWS ON HUMAN RESPONSIBILITY TOWARD CREATION

Theology is the major issue in the current debate about how to view the physical environment. There are at least three inadequate theological perspectives in the culture today. First is the equality view, often associated with St. Francis of Assisi, declaring all aspects of God's physical creation equal; there is no difference between the birds and humans. Legends about Francis depict him preaching to the birds and giving counsel to a wolf that threatens a small town in Italy. Biblically, the particulars of God's creation are not equal. Genesis 1 and 2 make it clear that humans are the crown of God's creation. Humans are the only ones who bear His image. Jesus did not die for birds; He died for human beings.

Second is pantheism, the view that all reality is one; all is God, and God is all. Pantheists reason that California redwoods should not be cut down because the trees are god. They also reason that whales should be saved because animals are god. Such is the pantheistic position reflected by many celebrities, the Gaia hypothesis, and the entire New Age worldview. The Bible does teach the presence of God everywhere (e.g., Ps. 139), but rejects the idea that *all* is God. He created all things and is above and beyond His physical creation. Pantheism is an unacceptable, unbiblical position.

Third is a commitment to platonic dichotomy, i.e., the idea that the spiritual world is all that is important, and the material world has no value to God or to us as His disciples. This philosophy views the world as passing away, and so it does not matter whether we treat it well or abuse it. Again, Scripture will not support this idea. The Bible details the goodness of God's creation (e.g., Gen. 1—2; 1 Tim. 4:4). It is wrong to view God's physical creation as unimportant. Furthermore, the physical body is of such importance to God that He will one day resurrect it (Rev. 20:5; 1 Thess. 4:16).

BIBLICAL PRINCIPLES FOR A PROPER VIEW OF THE ENVIRONMENT

A proper biblical view of the physical creation begins with a proper view of God. The challenge is to keep in balance God's transcendence and His immanence. God's transcendence focuses on His radical separateness from creation; He is both above and beyond His physical world. God's immanence focuses on His presence in His physical world. To stress His immanence at the expense of His transcendence is to land in pantheism where everything is god. To stress His transcendence at the expense of His immanence could lead to viewing the physical world as insignificant and a tool for exploitation. Neither is satisfactory nor God-honoring. We need to strike a balance between God's transcendence and His immanence, between His intimate involvement in all aspects of His physical creation (Ps. 139) and His radical distinction from creation. While creation is finite, limited, and dependent, He is infinite, unlimited, and self-sufficient.[4]

Second, to view the physical creation rightly, we need a proper view of humans. The Bible declares human uniqueness. This book has made much of humans as image-bearers of God with communion status. No other physical part of God's world can claim this status (Gen. 1:26-30). As argued in chapter 10, Genesis 2:15 is the corrective to dominion exploitation. Humans are to serve and watch lovingly over God's creation. We are God's stewards of His creation. He has the sovereignty; we have the dominion.

Human beings are both interdependent with the rest of creation and unique within it because we alone bear His image and have stewardship over the earth. Christians frequently forget our interdependence with the rest of God's world. Our daily existence depends on water, sun, and air. There is indeed a global ecosystem.[5] It matters how we treat the water, the trees, and the animals. If they are harmed, so are we.

Francis Schaeffer also argued that humans have two relationships—one upward and one downward. The upward is the personal relationship with God, a relationship not enjoyed by the rest of the created order. Downward is the "creaturely" relationship with the rest of the created order (Gen. 2:7; Job 34:14-15). As with most issues, the struggle is to maintain a balance. We tend to highlight the upward relationship to the virtual exclusion of the downward, resulting in horrific neglect or ruthless exploitation of the physical world. Or we tend to highlight the downward to the virtual exclusion of the upward. The gross error of the evolutionary hypothesis sees humans as the product of the impersonal force of natural selection, not of God's purposeful design.[6]

Third, the nonhuman creation is of great significance to God. He created the physical world as a deliberate act and takes pleasure in it. Note 1 Timothy 4:4: "For everything created by God is good, and nothing is to be rejected if it is received with gratitude." Psalm 104:31 also records God rejoicing in His works. The point is, if the physical world is of importance to God, then it must also be to us—His creatures (Job 39:1-2; Col. 1:16; Ps. 19:1-4).

As Ron Sider points out, it is likewise imperative to note that God has a covenant, not only with humans but also with the nonhuman creation. After the Flood, God made a covenant with the physical creation: "Behold, I Myself do establish My covenant with you, and with your descendants after you; and with every living creature that is with you, the birds, the cattle, and every beast of the earth with you; of all that comes out of the ark" (Gen. 9:9-10).[7] The physical world has dignity, worth, and value quite apart from its service to humanity.

Incredibly, God's plan for redemption has a cosmic quality to it. As Sider states, "This fact provides a crucial foundation for building a Christian theology for an environmental age."[8] The biblical hope that the whole created order, including the material world of bodies and rivers and trees, will be part of the kingdom confirms that the created order is good and important. Romans 8:19-23 demonstrates that at Christ's return the groaning of creation will cease, for the creation will be transformed: "The creation itself will be liberated from its bondage to decay and brought into the glorious freedom of the children of God" (v. 21 NIV).

THE MOTIVATION FOR GOOD STEWARDSHIP

Since we are God's stewards over His creation, what should be our motivation? Are we good stewards for *pragmatic* reasons or for *moral* reasons? The pragmatic view posits that we should be good stewards over

God's world because our very survival depends on it. For example, if we farm the hills irresponsibly, we will lose topsoil and harm our ability to produce food. If we wantonly kill snakes, eventually we will be overrun by rodents. If we mine copper irresponsibly, we will cause horrendous erosion. If we burn the rainforests, we pollute the air and destroy oxygen-producing trees, which in turn will threaten our supply of oxygen. But the Bible rejects this motive for good stewardship.

Instead, Scripture implores humans to exercise good stewardship over the physical world because to do so demonstrates honor and respect for God's created order. The physical creation should not be exploited because it is morally wrong to misuse God's created order. Having God's perspective, we responsibly farm, we do not wantonly destroy animal life, we responsibly mine copper, and we cease burning the rainforests because we respect and honor what God has honored and respected. We show honor to the physical world with which God has a covenant relationship. Christians should, therefore, be the leaders in responsible environmentalism. As God's theocratic stewards, we represent Him when we honor His physical world.

THE ENVIRONMENTAL SOLUTION

Francis Schaeffer argues that the church needs to be a "pilot plant" where the proper relationships between human beings and the physical world are modeled.[9] The church, he states, must be a place "where men can see in our congregations and missions a substantial healing of all divisions, the alienations, man's rebellion has produced."[10] A macroplan for reconciliation would involve five dimensions.

Humans Properly Related to God

For any type of reconciliation to occur, humans must trust Jesus Christ for salvation. The apostle Paul referred to his ministry as one of "reconciliation" (2 Cor. 5:18)—reconciling God and humanity through the finished work of Jesus Christ. Humans will never exercise proper God-honoring stewardship without first being reconciled to Him through Christ.

Humans Properly Related to Self

Humans must see themselves as God sees them—of infinite value as creatures and, in Christ, as redeemed. Because we have God's view of ourselves, we have proper respect for the body as eternally significant. A mark of the redeemed Christian is a commitment to care for and respect one's body. It belongs to God, and to allow it to be an instrument of sin or to treat it with disrespect is to say something about God, for He created and redeemed it. The Christian is no longer independent but forever dependent on the Lord who purchased him (Rom. 12:1-2; 1 Cor. 6:19-20).

Humans Properly Related to Other Humans

Because we now have Christ's mind, Christians view other humans through God's eyes. Christians treat all humans with respect, realizing shared creatureliness and shared value as image-bearers of God. This behavior is at the heart of Jesus' command to love God with heart, soul, mind, and strength and our neighbors as ourselves. The Good Samaritan story powerfully illustrates *how* one loves one's neighbor (Luke 10:30-37). All humans, redeemed and unredeemed, are of value and worth to God.

Humans Properly Related to Nature

Humans are to treat all aspects of God's physical creation with respect and honor. If all of God's creation is "good," then His disciples must have the same regard He has. It is ethically wrong to destroy wantonly what God has created. The nonhuman creation serves humans; that is the point of having dominion status. But humans are God's stewards representing Him. Stewardship also implies accountability—to Him.

Nature Properly Related to Nature

Romans 8:20-23 clarifies the phrase in verse 22, "the whole creation groans"; it awaits the return of Jesus when it will be restored. Then nature will be properly related to nature, and the horrific consequences of human sin that wreak havoc on the physical creation (Gen. 3) will end.

Christians must be at the forefront of the ecology movement so that God's glory is not preempted by a narrow humanistic agenda or an "antihuman" value system endemic to modern pantheism. We must not conclude that the earth is good and humanity evil. Also, we must not conclude that being concerned about the environment makes one an advocate of some form of pantheism or the Gaia hypothesis. The beauty and complexity of the earth are God's good gifts. We must cultivate respect and honor for God's physical creation. We are His stewards, and He is watching!

FOR FURTHER DISCUSSION

1. In the chapter's introduction, the author cites several wrong views of the relationship between humans and the physical environment. What is the Gaia hypothesis?
2. Explain each of the following inadequate views of the environment:
    * St. Francis of Assisi's view
    * Pantheism
    * Platonic dichotomy
3. Explain the three biblical principles for understanding God's perspective on the environment:
    * A proper view of God
    * A proper view of humans
    * A proper view of nature
4. Motivation for proper stewardship of the environment is critical. Explain the difference between pragmatic motivation and moral motivation.
5. Relying on Francis Schaeffer, the author proposes an "environmental solution" that consists of five levels. Explain each level:
    * Humans properly related to God
    * Humans having a proper view of self
    * Humans properly related to other humans
    * Humans properly related to nature
    * Nature properly related to nature

NOTES

CHAPTER 1
ETHICS: AN INTRODUCTION

1. R. C. Sproul, *Ethics and the Christian* (Wheaton, Ill.: Tyndale House, 1986), 9-22.
2. The Kinsey report was a massive human sexual behavior study conducted by Alfred Kinsey and first published in 1948. The report remains very controversial, and Kinsey's data collection methods have been called into question many times.
3. Erwin Lutzer, *The Necessity of Ethical Absolutes* (Dallas, Tex.: Probe, 1981), 14.

CHAPTER 2
ETHICAL OPTIONS FOR THE CHRISTIAN

1. James P. Eckman, "Preparing for the Postmodern Challenge," *Grace Tidings* (November 1997), 1.
2. Erwin Lutzer, *The Necessity of Ethical Absolutes* (Dallas, Tex.: Probe, 1981), 24.
3. Louis P. Pojman, *Ethics: Discovering Right and Wrong* (Belmont, Calif.: Wadsworth, 1995), 35.
4. Joseph Fletcher, *Situation Ethics* (Philadelphia: Westminster, 1966). This book was revised in 1997. Controversial at its first printing, the work remains debatable for its thesis that some acts (lying, murder) may be morally right depending on the circumstances.
5. Lutzer, *The Necessity of Ethical Absolutes*, 24-39.
6. B. F. Skinner, *Beyond Freedom and Dignity* (New York: Knopf, 1971), 231.
7. Lutzer, *The Necessity of Ethical Absolutes*, 70.
8. Bill Crouse, *Abortion and Human Value* (Dallas, Tex.: Probe, 1979), 1-4.
9. Anthony Hoekema, *Created in God's Image* (Grand Rapids: Eerdmans, 1986).
10. Francis Schaeffer and C. Everett Koop, *Whatever Happened to the Human Race?* (Old Tappan, N.J.: Revell, 1979), 153.

CHAPTER 3
HOW SHOULD A CHRISTIAN RELATE TO CULTURE?

1. Robert E. Webber, *The Secular Saint: A Case for Evangelical Social Responsibility* (Grand Rapids: Zondervan, 1979).
2. Ibid.

CHAPTER 4
ABORTION

1. Section 1531 (b), *The Partial-Birth Abortion Ban Act* (HR 1833) as vetoed by President William Clinton on April 10, 1996.
2. Paul and John Feinberg, *Ethics for a Brave New World* (Wheaton, Ill.: Crossway Books, 1993), 58.
3. Ibid., 71-72.
4. Marvin Olasky and Joel Belz, *Whirled Views* (Wheaton, Ill.: Crossway Books, 1997), 27.

CHAPTER 5
EUTHANASIA

1. Joseph Fletcher, *Situation Ethics* (Philadelphia: Westminster, 1966), 156-157.
2. James Manney and John C. Blattner, "Infanticide: Murder or Mercy," *Journal of Christian Nursing* (Summer 1985), 10-14.

CHAPTER 6
BIOETHICS

1. See the discussion on human development in Paul and John Feinberg, *Ethics for a Brave New World* (Wheaton, Ill.: Crossway Books, 1993).
2. Francis Schaeffer, *How Should We Then Live?* (Old Tappan, N.J.: Revell, 1976), chapter 12.
3. Russell Hittinger, "A Crisis of Legitimacy," *First Things* (November 1996), 26.
4. Carl Henry, *Christian Personal Ethics* (Grand Rapids: Eerdmans, 1957), 210.
5. Wray Herbert, "The Politics of Biology," *US News and World Report* (April 21, 1997), 72-80.

CHAPTER 7
HUMAN SEXUALITY

1. See Allen P. Ross, *Creation and Blessing: A Guide to the Study and Exposition of Genesis* (Grand Rapids: Baker, 1988), 117-129; Raymond C. Ortlund, Jr., "Male-Female Equality and Male Headship," in John Piper and Wayne Grudem, general editors, *Recovering Biblical Manhood and Womanhood* (Wheaton, Ill.: Crossway Books, 1991), 95-112.
2. Paul and John Feinberg, *Ethics for a Brave New World* (Wheaton, Ill.: Crossway Books, 1993), 199-201.
3. Jeffrey Satinover, *Homosexuality and the Politics of Truth* (Grand Rapids: Baker, 1996), 78-81.
4. Ibid., 16-17.
5. See the helpful article by Wray Herbert, "The Politics of Biology," *US News and World Report* (April 21, 1997), 72-80.
6. Letha Scanzoni and Virginia Mollenkott, *Is the Homosexual My Neighbor?* (New York: Harper, 1978). The book is actually a pro-gay theology text.

7. Don Baker, *Beyond Rejection* (Portland, Ore.: Multnomah, 1985). This book is must reading for the church, providing the balance of truth and compassion so needed on this issue.
8. Exodus is a worldwide interdenominational Christian organization focused on helping Christians minister to those affected by homosexuality. For more information, visit their web site at www.exodus-international.org or call 888-264-0877.

CHAPTER 8
THE CHRISTIAN AND POLITICS

1. Charles Colson, *Kingdoms in Conflict* (Grand Rapids: Zondervan, 1987), 109-121.
2. C. E. B. Cranfield, "The Christian's Political Responsibility According to the New Testament," *Scottish Journal of Theology* 15 (1962), 179.
3. Ibid., 176-192.
4. See the United States Constitution, Article 2, Section 4.
5. Lynn Buzzard, "Civil Disobedience," *Eternity* (January 1987), 19-25.
6. Cranfield, "The Christian's Political Responsibility," 185.
7. Charles Colson, "The Political Illusion," *Moody Monthly* (October 1994), 22-25.
8. Quoted in Bob Reynold, "Onward Christian Voters," *Moody Monthly* (September/October 1996), 23-25.

CHAPTER 9
THE ETHICAL CHALLENGE OF WAR AND
CAPITAL PUNISHMENT

1. Peter Craigie, *The Problem of War in the Old Testament* (Grand Rapids: Zondervan, 1978), 58.
2. Charles Ryrie, *You Mean the Bible Teaches That . . .* (Chicago: Moody, 1974), 30.
3. John Drescher, "Why Christians Shouldn't Carry Swords," *Christianity Today* (November 7, 1984), 17.
4. Norman Geisler, *Christian Ethics* (Grand Rapids: Baker, 1989), 223.
5. John Stott, *Involvements* (Grand Rapids: Zondervan, 1985), 44.
6. Drescher, "Why Christians Shouldn't Carry Swords," *Christianity Today*, 23.
7. Ibid., 21-22.
8. *The Complete Writings of Menno Simons, Circa 1496-1561*, ed. John C. Wenger, trans. Leonard Verduin (Scottsdale, Pa.: Herald Press, 1956), 42-43.
9. Geisler, *Christian Ethics*, 225.
10. Ibid., 220-228.
11. Ryrie, *You Mean the Bible Teaches That . . .* , 26-27.
12. John Eidsmoe, *God and Caesar* (Wheaton, Ill.: Crossway Books, 1989), 200.

CHAPTER 10
THE ETHICS OF WORK AND RACE

1. John A. Bernbaum and Simon A. Steer, *Why Work?* (Grand Rapids: Baker, 1986), 6-7.

2. See Arthur Holmes, *Contours of a World View* (Grand Rapids: Eerdmans, 1983), 219; Stanley Cramer and Edwin L. Herr, *Career Guidance and Counseling Through the Life Span* (Boston: Little Brown, 1979), 387.
3. Holmes, *Contours of a World View*, 216.
4. Allen P. Ross, *Creation and Blessing: A Guide to the Study and Exposition of Genesis* (Grand Rapids: Baker, 1988), 215.
5. Ibid.
6. Ibid., 217.
7. Ibid., 218.
8. Charles Ryrie, *You Mean the Bible Teaches That . . .* (Chicago: Moody, 1974), 60.

CHAPTER 11
THE CHRISTIAN, THE ARTS, AND ENTERTAINMENT

1. Peter Angeles, *Dictionary of Philosophy* (New York: Harper and Row, 1981), 51.
2. These principles are deduced from a seminar presented on the campus of Grace University by Dr. Howard Hendricks of Dallas Theological Seminary entitled "Creativity in Ministry," in the summer of 1992. Also see Arthur Holmes, *Contours of a World View* (Grand Rapids: Eerdmans, 1983), 206-210.
3. Gordon Jackson, "Evangelicals and the Arts: Divorce or Reconciliation?" *Spectrum* (Summer 1976), 17-19.
4. Quoted in Frank E. Gaebelein, "Toward a Biblical View of Aesthetics," *Christianity Today* (August 30, 1968), 5.
5. Francis Schaeffer, *Art and the Bible* (Downers Grove, Ill.: InterVarsity, 1974), 17.
6. Philip Yancey, *I Was Just Wondering* (Grand Rapids: Eerdmans, 1989), 3.
7. Schaeffer, *Art and the Bible*, 17.
8. Gaebelein, "Toward a Biblical View of Aesthetics," *Christianity Today*, 5.
9. H. R. Rookmaaker, *Art Needs No Justification* (Downers Grove, Ill.: InterVarsity, 1978), 31.
10. Schaeffer, *Art and the Bible*, 24.
11. Gaebelein, "Toward a Biblical View of Aesthetics," *Christianity Today*, 5.
12. Ibid., 13.
13. Rookmaaker, *Art Needs No Justification*, 18.
14. Calvin Seerveld, *A Christian Critique of Art and Literature* (Toronto: Association for the Advancement of Christian Scholarship, 1968), 28-29.
15. Richard Zoglin, "Is TV Ruining Our Children?" *Time* (June 19, 1989), 75.
16. Ibid.
17. Clement Walchshauser, *Fundamentalist Journal* (October 1984), 12.
18. Linda Winder, "TV: What It's Doing to Your Children," *Living Today* (March-May 1987), 5.
19. Quentin Schultze, *Television: Manna from Hollywood?* (Grand Rapids: Zondervan, 1986), 150.

CHAPTER 12
THE CHRISTIAN AND THE ENVIRONMENT

1. Ronald J. Sider, "Redeeming the Environmentalists," *Christianity Today* (June 21, 1993), 26.

2. Rosemary Ruether, *Gaia and God: An Ecofeminist Theology of Earth Healing* (New York: Harper, 1993).

3. Francis Schaeffer, *Pollution and the Death of Man: The Christian View of Ecology* (Wheaton: Tyndale, 1970).

4. Sider, "Redeeming the Environmentalists," *Christianity Today*, 28.

5. Ibid.

6. Schaeffer, *Pollution and the Death of Man*, 47-61.

7. Sider, "Redeeming the Environmentalists," 29.

8. Ibid.

9. Schaeffer, *Pollution and the Death of Man*, 81-93.

10. Ibid., 82.

Bibliography

CHAPTER 1

Lutzer, Erwin. *The Necessity of Ethical Absolutes*. Dallas: Probe, 1981.

Sproul, R. C. *Ethics and the Christian*. Wheaton: Tyndale, 1986.

CHAPTER 2

Berkouwer, G. C. *Man: Image of God*. Grand Rapids: Eerdmans, 1962.

Crouse, Bill. *Abortion and Human Value*. Dallas: Probe, 1979.

Hoekema, Anthony. *Created in God's Image*. Grand Rapids: Eerdmans, 1986.

Pojman, Louis P. *Ethics: Discovering Right and Wrong*. Belmont, Calif.: Wadsworth, 1995.

Schaeffer, Francis, and Koop, C. Everett. *Whatever Happened to the Human Race?* Old Tappan, N.J.: Revell, 1979.

Skinner, B. F. *Beyond Freedom and Dignity*. New York: Knopf, 1971.

CHAPTER 3

Niebuhr, H. Richard. *Christ and Culture*. New York: Harper, 1951.

Webber, Robert E. *The Secular Saint: A Case for Evangelical Social Responsibility*. Grand Rapids: Zondervan, 1979.

CHAPTER 4

Feinberg, Paul and Feinberg, John. *Ethics for a Brave New World*. Wheaton, Ill.: Crossway Books, 1993.

Wilkie, John. *Handbook on Abortion*. Cincinnati: Hiltz, 1971.

CHAPTER 5

Fletcher, Joseph. *Situation Ethics*. Philadelphia: Westminster, 1966.

CHAPTER 6

Henry, Carl. *Christian Personal Ethics*. Grand Rapids: Eerdmans, 1957.

Schaeffer, Francis. *How Should We Then Live?* Old Tappan, N.J.: Revell, 1976.

CHAPTER 7

Baker, Don. *Beyond Rejection*. Portland, Ore.: Multnomah, 1985.

Piper, John, and Grudem, Wayne. *Recovering Biblical Manhood and Womanhood*. Wheaton, Ill.: Crossway Books, 1991.

Ross, Allen P. *Creation and Blessing: A Guide to the Study and Exposition of Genesis*. Grand Rapids: Baker, 1988.

Satinover, Jeffrey. *Homosexuality and the Politics of Truth*. Grand Rapids: Baker, 1996.

Scanzoni, Letha, and Mollenkott, Virginia. *Is the Homosexual My Neighbor?* New York: Harper, 1978.

CHAPTER 8

Colson, Charles. *Kingdoms in Conflict*. Grand Rapids: Zondervan, 1987.

CHAPTER 9

Clouse, Robert G., ed. *War: Four Christian Views*. Downers Grove, Ill.: InterVarsity, 1981.

Craigie, Peter. *The Problem of War in the Old Testament*. Grand Rapids: Zondervan, 1978.

Eidsmoe, John. *God and Caesar*. Wheaton, Ill.: Crossway Books, 1989.

Geisler, Norman. *Christian Ethics*. Grand Rapids: Baker, 1989.

Ryrie, Charles. *You Mean the Bible Teaches That . . .* Chicago: Moody, 1974.

Stott, John. *Involvements*. Grand Rapids: Zondervan, 1985.

Wells, Ronald, ed. *The Wars of America: Christian Views*. Grand Rapids: Eerdmans, 1981.

CHAPTER 10

Bernbaum, John A., and Steer, Simon. *Why Work?* Grand Rapids: Baker, 1986.

Cramer, Stanley H., and Herr, Edwin L. *Career Guidance and Counseling Through the Life Span*. Boston: Little, Brown, 1979.

Engstrom, Ted W., and Juroe, David J. *The Work Trap*. Old Tappan, N.J.: Revell, 1979.

Holmes, Arthur F. *Contours of a World View*. Grand Rapids: Eerdmans, 1983.

CHAPTER 11

Rookmaaker, H. R. *Art Needs No Justification*. Downers Grove, Ill.: InterVarsity, 1978.

Schaeffer, Francis. *Art and the Bible*. Downers Grove, Ill.: InterVarsity, 1974.

Schaeffer, Franky. *Addicted to Mediocrity: 20th-Century Christians and the Arts*. Westchester, Ill.: Cornerstone, 1981.

Schultze, Quentin. *Television: Manna from Hollywood?* Grand Rapids: Zondervan, 1986.

Seerveld, Calvin. *A Christian Critique of Art and Literature*. Toronto: The Association for the Advancement of Christian Scholarship, 1968.

Yancey, Philip. *I Was Just Wondering*. Grand Rapids: Eerdmans, 1989.

CHAPTER 12

Ruether, Rosemary. *Gaia and God: An Ecofeminist Theology of Earth Healing*. New York: Harper, 1993.

Schaeffer, Francis. *Pollution and the Death of Man: The Christian View of Ecology*. Wheaton, Ill.: Tyndale, 1970.

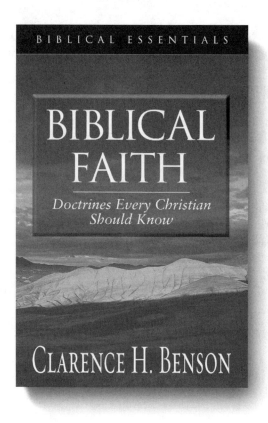

BIBLICAL FAITH:
DOCTRINES EVERY CHRISTIAN SHOULD KNOW
CLARENCE H. BENSON

Why do Christians study doctrine? You might say our faith depends on it. In a culture that promotes a variety of religions and argues that all are equally valid, it is essential that Christians know doctrine. Without sound doctrine, our faith is in danger of being distorted or destroyed. In *Biblical Faith*, Dr. Benson offers a concise, straightforward explanation of twelve basic doctrines. The book begins by discussing what evangelical Christians believe about Scripture and then explores doctrines from Creation and the Fall to heaven and hell. The most profound truths of the Bible are described in a way that is clear and easy to understand.

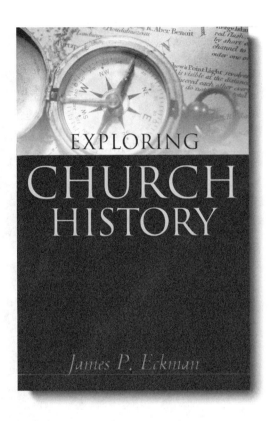

EXPLORING CHURCH HISTORY
JAMES P. ECKMAN

When we study church history, we are learning about more than just names and dates. We are exploring our own Christian heritage. And as we study the past, we also prepare ourselves for the future, because many contemporary issues are not new at all. A study of church history also gives an accurate understanding of the complexities and richness of Christianity. The church has suffered much, but a thorough look at its past reinforces our conviction that the church will triumph. Dr. James Eckman leads readers through church history from the Pentecost to the present. This basic introduction, done chronologically, emphasizes the theological process and developing consensus within the church on what the Scriptures teach, as well as the institutional development of the church.

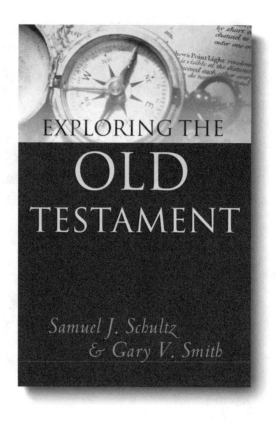

EXPLORING THE OLD TESTAMENT
SAMUEL J. SCHULTZ AND GARY V. SMITH

It is imperative for every growing Christian to study all of the Bible. In *Exploring the Old Testament,* Samuel Schultz and Gary Smith survey the content of the Old Testament so that readers will understand each book's events and themes. Chapters conclude with projects, questions, and exploration activities that not only test readers' grasp of the materials but also provide opportunity for more detailed and intensive study. This book acquaints people with the Old Testament's major divisions and its amazing unity as a whole. Both authors are well-equipped to guide readers through the Old Testament. Schultz is Professor Emeritus of Bible and Theology at Wheaton Graduate School, and Smith is Professor of Old Testament at Midwestern Baptist Theological Seminary.

EXPLORING THE NEW TESTAMENT
WALTER M. DUNNETT

Exploring the New Testament takes a survey approach that will deepen your knowledge of God and enrich your understanding of the Bible. Readers will gain an overview of the entire New Testament, consider the respective writers and their work, and understand the purpose, outline, main content, and leading features of each New Testament book. All of these elements lay a solid foundation for understanding the message and revelation of Jesus Christ. The chapters end with application activities and discussion questions. Author Walter Dunnett served on the faculty of Northwestern College.

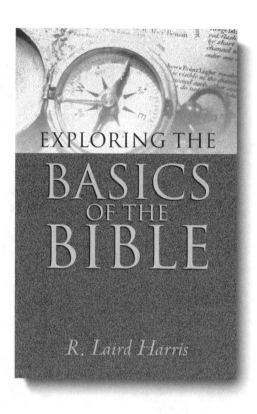

EXPLORING THE BASICS OF THE BIBLE
R. LAIRD HARRIS

The Scriptures are God's Word to us. We should personally read them, study them, meditate upon them, and most of all, practice them. But the first step to a truly enriching study of the Bible is understanding the basics behind its writing. R. Laird Harris's introductory book explores important questions that many wonder about: Who wrote the Bible? How was it written? Why should I believe that it is God's Word? What about its seeming contradictions and problems? All these topics and more are covered in this thorough treatment of the truth about the Bible. The book concludes with chapters on study helps and Bible study methods, as well as a list of resources for enrichment. Harris is widely known and respected for his biblical scholarship, as well as his past teaching and leadership at Covenant Theological Seminary.

EVIDENCE AND TRUTH:
FOUNDATIONS FOR CHRISTIAN TRUTH
ROBERT J. MORGAN

How do we know that Christianity is true? How do we respond to doubters who say that our faith is only about fictional stories and unfounded feelings? In *Evidence and Truth*, Robert Morgan takes readers step-by-step through the well-documented historical and physical evidence that supports the claims of Christianity. He deals with such topics as the resurrection of Christ, the complexity of creation, the reliability of the Bible, and the changed lives of believers. Whether the reader is looking for personal answers or wants to be prepared to answer a friend, this book will help. *Evidence and Truth* offers a solid intellectual basis from which the reader can take a step of faith and experience the ultimate assurance that comes from God's Spirit. A graduate of Columbia International University and Wheaton College Graduate School, Morgan pastored for nearly twenty-five years and has authored several books.

Since 1930

Evangelical Training Association

THE MINISTRIES OF EVANGELICAL TRAINING ASSOCIATION

(ETA)

Experienced – Founded in 1930.
Doctrinally Dependable – Conservative and evangelical theology.
Educationally Sound – Engaging all adult learning styles.
Thoroughly Field-Tested – Used by a global constituency.
Recommended – Officially endorsed by denominations and schools.
Ministry Driven – Committed to quality training resources for equipping lay volunteers to serve Christ more effectively in the church.
Affordable – Attractive and reasonably priced.

For many local ministries, the most important step to an effective lay leadership training program is locating and implementing an inspiring, motivational system of instruction. ETA curriculum is available as traditional classroom courses, audio and video seminars, audio and video CD-ROM packages, and other resources for your classroom teaching or personal study.

Contact ETA today for free information and a 20-minute video presentation. Request Information Packet: Crossway Partner.

EVANGELICAL TRAINING ASSOCIATION
110 Bridge Street • PO Box 327 • Wheaton, IL 60189
800-369-8291 • FAX 630-668-8437 • www.etaworld.org